GIVE ME YESTERDAY

Aet. 18

GIVE ME YESTERDAY

JAMES WILLIAMS

GWASG GOMER
1971

First published November 1971

SBN 85088125 0

'Oh God! put back Thy universe and give me yesterday'. *The Silver King* II. iv. Henry Arthur Jones & Herman. Lond. 1907.

Printed in Wales
by J. D. Lewis & Sons Ltd., Gwasg Gomer, Llandysul, Cardiganshire.

To Old Friends
the Quick and the Dead

PREFACE

THE nostalgic yearning for our yesterdays may be nothing more than a refusal to accept the future, and its probable way of life ; we see the future only darkly, but we see the past clearly in focus. Time, like a medieval alembic distils the past, leaving memory to select what it wishes to remember. That is why a book about one's early life is not objective ; it is a catalogue of prejudices, of illogical likes and dislikes. We instinctively remember the parts we wish to, discounting those which we do not. To return to the haunts of our childhood can be a saddening experience, everything is so much smaller than in our memory. Cottages we have known are in ruins, with trees usually ash or sycamore, growing out through the roofs ; footpaths, once well-trodden are overgrown, no welcoming smoke rises from the chimneys, and we hear no merry voices of children at play. When I returned recently to the *cwm* of my childhood, I found that alders, brambles, and blackthorn had taken possession of fertile fields where once I helped at haymaking. My favourite trout pools were effectively obscured by sucker alder growth, strands of barbed wire denied passage over the old stiles ' sticill ', the mill leat had been bulldozed, and drainage everywhere neglected. Even the springs where we had so often quenched our sweating thirst lying on our stomachs, with face immersed, both eyes wide open, had become through neglect little bogs or swamps. Many years had passed since comely maidens and grey-haired grannies had filled their pitchers with the good water of these wells. Around the dilapided cottages lilacs left undisturbed, had thriven mightily, while the laburnums were festooned with chains of golden glory. The natural beauty of the *cwm* was still breath-taking, but it no longer nourished the aesthetic cravings of its own inhabitants ; these had all left. I missed them and felt they should have been there. It was quite illogical to expect not to miss them, but they had lived unageing in my memory, and I have always loved them ; they were kind, also intelligent. I had chosen to forget that they too grew old along with us. At times like Longfellow's Acadians, they were ' Men whose lives glided on like rivers that water the woodlands, darkened by shadows of earth, but reflecting an image of heaven' ; but not at all times, for they had fire in their bellies, and they could always discover an injustice against which to fight, or a cause worthy of their support. Perhaps we should never go back—never undertake sentimental journeys—never return to the old school, the old college, the old home. I do not think so—for our whole life is a returning, well put in the ribald song popular with unregenerate undergraduates of my day,—

'Ashes to ashes and dust to dust
If whisky don't get you the women must
It's the bee that gets the honey,
That doesn't hang around the hive'.

So last year I returned on my own, for a while, '*am siwrnai*' to my childhood haunts, to walk and talk with ghosts. In so much as we shall all die, 'tis no bad thing before paying our debt, to see once more the places where it all began, and in between-times to do our best to find out what it's all been about. For me life has been on the whole great fun,—a perpetual challenge. I have enjoyed the living of it, and I unrepentantly do not feel greatly disposed to draw my last wages, in order to strum in Heaven, or stoke in Hell. Is there a third choice ? We see, if we see at all, through a glass darkly, and maybe there is nothing but Hamlet's 'undiscover'd country from whose bourn no traveller returns', but why worry when life this side of the border is so fascinating ?

CONTENTS

EARLY DAYS

I was born in a very old small stone-walled farm house in a *cwm* (narrow glen). A stone panel between the two upstairs windows announced that it had been rebuilt in 1789, an event which had no connexion with what was then taking place in France. The house was probably falling down, so it had to have a face-lift. Nature had so bountifully endowed this *cwm* with beauty, that man could add nothing, only try to maintain and improve its communications with the outside world. I was born before the midwife or the doctor had arrived, and weighed nearly ten pounds. As I look upon myself in a mirror, I think they may have underestimated my weight. We were a close-knit happy family for ' better is a dinner of herbs where love is, than a stalled ox and hatred therewith '. To help each other was a pleasure ; to be funny and outrageous was not frowned on by our parents, neither of whom was a fidfad. Father had a peculiarly pixilated sense of humour. He loved a practical joke. I learnt at a very early age how to turn mother's wrath into helpless laughter—by recounting to the company gathered round the table her scoldings, but exaggerating the trivial and reducing the serious nuances of her lecture.

I loved this *cwm* always, every part of it, its streams, its woods thickly carpeted by blue-bells and bilberry bushes, its slopes covered in summer with the blazing yellow of the broom and gorse ; its badgers, foxes, rabbits, wood-pigeons and brown trout in the river. Above all I loved the people who lived in stone houses close to the river side. Time has been indulgent, for I can still recall with sensuous delight with all of the five senses, smell, sight, hearing, taste, and touch. Of these the sense of smell acts as a catalyst to produce a flood of remembrances of my boyhood scene.

I think all country creatures, of whom I am one, and ever shall be, have a much keener and more discriminatory sense of smell than those born and bred in towns. I am grateful, that in spite of surgical treatment to my nose as a result of war-damage—my sense of smell has remained unimpaired. I feel sorry for those who come on the television screen to confess their complete inability to distinguish between butter and margarine ; they would not be such pitiable objects had they been brought up on good Welsh or Breton butter! I have just jotted down the scents and smells I liked and can still 'taste' in my mind. They are the fragrance in the dewy summer evenings, of the cabbage-red roses which grew in profusion in a hedgerow outside the cowshed, where mother playfully squirted the foamy creamy warm milk from one teat of the cow right into our wide-open mouths. Great fun, for sometimes she missed the mouth but got the eye. The hedge was composed of black and white thorn —the blossom of both yielding a heavy but attractive perfume. There were lilacs everywhere, which earned their keep by dispensing, what must surely rate as one of the most entrancing scents in all creation. Perhaps one day an enterprising newspaper will conduct an opinion poll on scents, in which case lilac would rank high—in the company of the most dewy perfume of the lilies of the valley which is like the bouquet of a superlative dessert wine. But for God's plenty of good friendly smell, give me new-mown hay, on the two successive evenings after it has been cut. The smells, as opposed to perfumes, associated with childhood which I like, are those arising from horses and cows when they come in from the wet and begin to steam ; the smells of various farmyard manures—which vary according to age. The smell of honest sweat from men working in the harvest fields—there is nothing repulsive about it—especially when Welsh absorbent woollen shirts are worn. We had two gardens, and in one was an old cottage, with masses of stocks and gilly-flowers, whose perfume suffused the still evening air, after the sun on its westward course had departed from this part of the garden. There were the old bronze, the yellows and the blood-red, each one with its individual scent, but blending together to lend enchantment to that part of the garden.

But all smells are not outside. Perhaps to hungry children the most attractive indoor smell was that of pig-fry on the day following a pig-sticking. We boys slept together in a large oak postered bed, underneath which apples were laid on old newspapers. The early eating ones had finished, so beneath the bed would be James Grieve, Lord Derby, Bramley Seedling, the *afal pren glas* (the green wood apple), most fragrant, tasty with a very juicy white flesh, Gascoigne's Scarlet, Charles Ross, Worcester Pearmain, Lane's Prince Albert, Newton Wonder, Jolly Beggar and others which had no other appellation than being coupled with the names of the persons who had given the scion to be grafted. Oddly enough we had no Cox's or Laxton's, but there was one small bush of Sturmer

Pippin. And of course there were no D'Arcy Spice that ugly looking Essex apple with a heavenly taste and flesh white as leprosy. I once became intoxicated in Italy after walking in empty wine vats—empty of grapes that is, but full of potent fumes. I wonder whether we slept slightly doped with this vast hoard of apples beneath and around us ?

Finally there was the leather covered Bible, which in 1823 had belonged to Henry Evans. It behaved like a barometer—strong smell when rain was nigh, but no smell when the weather was fair. It lay on part of the chimney-breast on the shelf caused by the corbelling, and close to our noses. I still have this volume, but central-heating combined with modern amenities seem to have blunted its sharp prophetic weather sense.

The water meadow in front of the house was bordered by a trout stream, with pools in which we bathed and learnt to swim a few strokes. To this day as a result of this untutored empirical method, I swim with a strange blend of the breast and the side stroke. It has served me happily all my life. I taught it to my daughter, and to one of my two sons—who, I am glad to say are perfectly content with it. It is not a fast stroke, but the swimmer can see clearly where he is going, unlike the back-strokers who see only where they come from. In this *cwm* were the ruins of a woollen factory, with its water wheel, a pathetic survival, several weavers cottages, the walls of which are still standing, and when I was a boy beds of teasels grew just outside each one. These, I think were Fuller's teasels, whose heads were composed of a multitude of barbs, hence their use for teaseling cloth, the universal *brethyn gwlad* of the time. The advent of the ' ready-made ' clothes killed the demand for the hand-woven cloth which would last a life-time, and started the depopulation of these lovely *cwms*, a movement which the opening of coal pits, and the processing of metals accelerated, for the men folk found better-paid work in industrial Wales. We shall be paying for the Industrial Revolution for quite a time yet.

Last year I measured some of these stone ruins. The stone walls were a yard thick. Inside was one room measuring 15 feet by 12 feet. The hearth was 6 feet leaving two nooks of 3 feet each on either side. About half of the living room had a loft with a ladder for access. This loft was lit by only one small window. The height outside to the eaves was 11 feet. The entrance door faced south. One of these weaver's cottages was known as Niniveh. It is incredible that in these dwellings were reared families of twelve or more. Of course the more children a weaver had—the more free labour to process the cloth. It was a hard existence, but it was no doubt leavened by love, and an early acceptance of the inevitability of hardship. For these cotters the highlight of the week, and of their lives, was the Sunday attendance at their local chapel. Without this cultural relief, dulness could erode, even destroy the family harmony.

There was always a well, with a good spring of clear drinking water nearby. Every dwelling had an orchard of apple, damson and plum trees, and not more than a stone's throw was the quarry where the stone to build the cottage had been obtained. Every house, large or small, in the *cwm* had its own stone quarry, the location of which might have dictated the precise site of the building. The long bitter-sweet damsons made wonderful jam, and also, a delightfully astringent deep maroon coloured liquid to pour over a Sunday dinner rice pudding. There were also, without fail, the elder trees, the flower of which was made into a most palatable wine, which is still considered when heated, to be a specific against all the ills of the chest particularly bronchitis or pneumonia. The elderberry too, made a rich ruby wine, which somehow masqueraded as a non-intoxicant wine, whereas it packed a punch like the kick of a mule. My mother brewed beer regularly, but she and her neighbours also made dozens of bottles of wine,—cowslip, parsnip, elderberry, elderflower, damson, bullus *eirin*, dandelion and the most glorious of them all—gorse flower. This was the Welsh tampoy, gorse flowers being used instead of gilliflowers. The gorse petals were picked when the sun beat fiercely on them, and taken hurriedly home before dusk fell, and put into the vat. Like our home-brewed beer, the gorse flower wine left no hangover, but the effect of a few glasses was to make one feel Olympian—one of the gods. Years ago the widow of an old rector, and mother of a dear school friend of mine, gave me two or three tots, before starting my ten mile mountain drive home. Never have I negotiated a dangerous twisting road so fast or so well—at least I thought so. Instead of needing the saving hand of God, I was God, sitting in a chariot which obeyed my slightest unuttered command. There was in that golden wine something far more uplifting than alcohol—and much more ennobling. It was endowed with all the qualities of a great wine,—colour richly Samian, a fragrance which met your nostrils with magic, and a taste which seduced the critical faculties of the tongue and membranes. This golden gorseflower wine, was surely greater than the wines of antiquity, those of Chios, Lesbos, Peparethos, Thasos, and Samos. It combined all the best qualities of these, with those of Biblical wines, the Schecher, the Tirose, the Mimsach and the Schemahrin. It uplifted the human spirit, which then looked down upon itself, and was satisfied with what it saw. Could it have been made from a long-lost recipe for the milk of paradise, re-discovered on the slopes of Precelly mountains in Pembrokeshire ?

My earliest recollection goes back to the hay harvest at our neighbour's farm when I was 4 years and 3 months. I cannot lay claim to the incredible memory feats of Compton Mackenzie, but I still remember this harvest time vividly, for I was allowed to carry a small jar of beer, and a cup, to the men working in the haggard and hayfields. I had served one lone worker with his drink, when curiosity made me taste the beer. I found it palatable, and so drank more, and again more, and then some, with the inevitable consequence of passing out into drunken oblivion. I was discovered fast asleep against a cock of hay—and was taken home to sleep it off. Apparently there were no ill effects, but later that summer, I was drunk again after helping Marged our neighbour, with the honey and the mead. I swallowed off and on, lots of very good honey—and drank sip after sip of the delicious mead. I knew it was the heavenliest beverage I had hitherto tasted, but my experience was about as limited as my discretion. Then suddenly I said I was going home, only two small fields away, for I was being enveloped by a billowing cloud of nausea. I was only half way home when I began to vomit, and for a time apparently could not stop—and then I passed out. Marged who had anxiously watched my erratic homeward progress, rushed to salvage me. She was very concerned. To this day I do not like honey, and mead not at all, despite the fact that it was a royal beverage among the early Welsh. King Arthur had a mead-cellar with flagons of mead, and golden goblets out of which to drink it. Hywel Dda's mead-cellar in Whitland, Pembrokeshire, was in charge of a senior official, the Steward of the Household. The defeat and slaughter of the Welsh at the battle of Cattraeth, has been attributed to the incapacitating effect of the mead they drank to excess, before battle was joined. Pale mead had been their feast, and proved a poison. The Anglo-Saxons likewise cared deeply for mead, and early in that grand old poem *Beowulf*, we are introduced to the ' medo-earn ' the Mead-hall. Later we hear of the medo-benc, mead-bench, medo-ful mead cup, medo-stig mead-path, and after over 2,000 lines, to medu-dream mead-joy. Perhaps I arrived at the mead-joy stage too early in life, for the thousands of Celts and Saxons who were addicted to mead, cannot have all been wrong.

I have also witnessed the potent effect of mead when drunk to excess by uninitiated adults. Once on the way home from school, I called at the house of Auntie Ann. She asked me to take a message to a neighbouring farm where the traction engine and threshing machine were at work. As I approached the stack yard I could hear no mellow hum of machinery nor the snorts of an engine admitting extra steam while taking up its load. The long leather fanbelt had stopped and was hanging limp, the head of steam had declined and the driver and his fireman were fast asleep, with several others leaning against a stack. They resembled a frieze of the Seven Sleepers of Effesos, and on their faces were expressions of great inward joy as if they were participants in tremendously exciting dreams.

Old Ben, Marged's father was a great character. He tended his bees without a veil, and also made his own skeps and hives which stood in the garden on a long stone shelf in a vast flower border. Any old metal hoops of convenient diameter, were used to hold the thatch which kept the rain out. He made a great ceremony of 'telling' the bees what was going on, emphasising with little taps by a big old key which he had for the purpose. Whatever he told them—it was not enough to prevent them swarming, and with as much rattling of tins as we could while running, we'd try to follow the swarm till it settled. Then just as soon as they had settled, Ben would unhurriedly come with his skep and take them home. Another colony to be housed, and in winter fed.

He was also deeply versed in the virtues of the herbs of the hedgerows, and herbal recipes for untold ills were available from him on request. Evan Evans was another herbalist, a great old character who believed that constant good health depended on a regular intake of a tisane of wood betony, which he called *cribau Sion Ffraed.* Sheaves of this herb were picked by him in summer and hung from the ceilings of his cottage. He fervently advised me never to be without a few leaves of this sovereign remedy in my pocket and to chew them at frequent intervals. This good old man was a deacon at our chapel, and his impromptu prayers were off-beat and mystical. No one doubted the absolute purity of his character.

But the time was approaching when I was to exchange the sweet freedom of living at home for a more constrained routine. In the

Summer term when I was just five, I was taken to the same local Board school that my mother had attended.

The school was situated on a hill, about 2 miles from home. Practically the whole journey to it was along footpaths, leafy lanes, over streams, through woods and fields, across the churchyard with its pound for straying beasts, its gigantic haunted hollow yew, then on to the foot of the hill. I suppose there was a pinder in charge of the pound, but I never knew who he was. He was probably the sexton who lived at the Inn close by. There were only three dwellings all the way from home to the classroom. One of them was occupied by Kitty, mother's aunt, and she was a fine old dear, always good for a red apple, a sweetie, or a Welsh cake. She had a parrot which had to be removed to outer darkness when the minister called, because of his f'c'sle vocabulary She took Hollands for her health's sake, adding sugar and hot water to the gin. My school was closed two years ago, for the policy of the Education mandarins, even in Wales where they should know better, is, to herd the children at collection points to be picked up like so many milk churns and taken in a bus to a big school in a town where they are exposed to urbanisation which is an insidious poison of the spirit. There some become smart Alecs, spivs, or what have you, but others wilt and do not develop in this alien atmosphere. The country educates, the town destroys. Small holdings have been abandoned because they are considered too far from a bus route. The bus-borne child of today knows little of the joys of eating ' bread and cheese ' off the white hawthorn, the ' bacon ' from the sweet-scented briar, as succulent and tender as young asparagus, the acid astringent sorrel leaves culled from the abundance which grew in damp patches in woods and by streams, the sweet cowslip petals and the pungently sweet gorse flowers ; beech-mast underneath the giant beeches in the churchyard ; crab apples, blackberries, bullus, all were ours and they were free. We made our own bows and arrows, crossbows, slings and catapults. In nearly every household there was a baby, and that meant lots of elastic tubing—bought by the yard—which was used to connect the teat to the baby's milk bottle. Lengths of this elastic would be tied to a Y fork cut from the hedgerow, and secured to a piece of soft leather, usually cut from a lady's kid glove. This held the pebble or marble. Constant practice made us experts in the use of these weapons, and often we would make a woodland fire to grill our bag—starlings covered with lice but plucked and gutted, a squab, a young rabbit. Life in the raw ? maybe, but part of a sane education.

For my first day at school I was dressed in a pair of white woollen shorts, a shirt of flannelette, and a little jacket. I was placed in the care of my eldest brother whom I embarrassed mightily, for as soon as the whistle was blown we formed into lines. This was the routine, wet or fine, and those who missed lines were automatically classified as unpunctual delinquents, and given a couple of strokes. The Headmaster gave the command—' Right turn, quick march '. I refused to budge and in a clear voice said ' Johnny shall I go ? ' He hurriedly said, ' Yes ', otherwise nothing would have moved me, apart from superior brute force, of which there was plenty around me. Mother had told me to do what my big brother said I was to do, and I had assimilated this lesson so thoroughly, that I felt no obligation to obey anyone else. But time came when I forgot to obey one of his commands. I must have been seven or eight, when my elder brother who had been charged with the care of our younger brother, a toddler in red frock and petticoats, brought him along to a field where I was happily tickling trout. Passing the buck neatly, he said that our mother had told him to get me to look after him. Then he went away, and I became so engrossed in what I was doing that I completely forgot my toddler brother, till I heard a cry and saw him fall from the bank into the stream. He was floating down with the current, the air in his petticoats keeping him afloat. I ran to the spot where the river was spanned by a plank foot bridge. Hooking my legs around it I dangled with my outstretched arms just touching the water. I fielded my brother who was in a dreadful state, but I could not get back on to the footbridge—so joining my voice to his I called for help. This fetched our elder brother who got us back on land. I felt terribly guilty and rushed away to hide in the gorse bushes near the house. At dusk the family were out calling, and finally I came back, not to a hiding, no, not even a scolding, but to be fêted as a hero, for I had saved a life. I have often teased this brother whose life I saved, by saying that I have always had doubts about the wisdom of fishing him out of the water on a summer's day of long ago.

The school was administered by a Board of Managers,—local notables, nearly all of whom were prominent Baptists. The overriding consideration of both the managers and the headmaster, was to secure a high average attendance, for the maintenance grant was geared to this. Thus, when the managers granted casual holidays, and these were many—they not only supported the Baptist cause, but safeguarded the sacred average attendance figure.

When the Baptist Association had their meetings at Penybryn or at one of the other local Baptist chapels, a full day's holiday was always declared. Half-days were allowed for the afternoon of a sale day at the farms of the parents of pupils at school. Occasionally in the day book, one reads that the harvest was backward, with many children consequently absent. As early as 1882 it had become usual to close the school for the day when the local Singing Festival was being held. In 1888, we have the very human entry for 25 June, 'This morning Mr. Williams late Chairman of the Board and Mr. W. Williams the present Vice-Chairman asked me to allow the children to stay at Penybryn to see Wombell's Menagerie passing to Kilgerran consequently school was not opened this morning'. The annual Hiring Fair at Cardigan on 10 November was always the occasion for a full day's holiday. I remember what excitement this fair brought with its tattoed lady, the swing-boats, the caravans, the giant Calliope of the Studt merry-go-round, and the huge traction engines gay in their bright brass and paint. The Studts still come to this Fair field every year, and I understand, they still own the field. Father used to win all sorts of clocks and ornaments at the 'hoopla' stall. The owner of the standing once gave him 5/- to go away. Local funerals meant a half day off. On 17 June 1891 the entry for the day informs us that the attendance was low because of two local Singing Festivals, one the Church of England, the other the Independents, but their combined might could not gain them officially even a half-day's holiday, whereas on the previous 2 March a full day's holiday had been granted on the occasion of the Baptist Singing Festival. Was this religious discrimination? I'm sure the Baptist managers did not think so. As the chosen sect, for such they considered themselves to be, they were disinclined to encourage Churchmen, who were wicked Tories anyway, or the Dissenters who stubbornly refused to accept the soul-saving virtue of baptism by immersion, which was available free at Penybryn and other conveniently near Baptist chapels. In those days denominational jealousy was as ludicrous as it was petty, but it was real.

1892 was an interesting year. On 8 February the day book informs us that a boy playing with a pistol sustained damage in his hand when it accidentally went off, two fingers having to be amputated. Lock-jaw set in, and in two weeks the boy was dead. On 15 July polling at Penybryn took place in the General Election—so no school. Throughout this month haymaking caused havoc with the attendance. This did not prevent a full day's holiday on 11 August, when Penybryn Baptist Sunday School went to Poppit for their annual outing, and five days later a day's holiday for Tyrhos Sunday School trip to Poppit. On October 11 there was no school because of the centenary celebrations of the Baptist Missionary Society at Cardigan. The afternoon of 21 October was a half-holiday because of an auction at a neighbouring farm, and 6 days later, there was another day's holiday because of the Harvest Festival at Penybryn and at Bridell. Events which called for holidays either full or half-days, were hay making, cattle shows, any Baptist activity, funerals, tea-parties, the official opening of the new Grammar School Cardigan 20 September 1898, the opening 2 October 1901, of Seion Baptist Chapel at Crymych, the Menagerie at Cardigan, or a snow storm. Longer closures occurred, when the Medical Officer advised, 4 weeks because of whooping cough in 1910, a week from 16 June in 1911 to celebrate the coronation of King George V, and in May 1913 the school was closed for a week because of measles. On 13 July 1911 Mrs. Morris, Broyan Mill, gave a tea party to all the children, and every child a mug to commemorate the Investiture of the Prince of Wales. The temperature in the school room in January and February 1912 was 38° because coal was being hoarded owing to the general fear of a strike. In 1914 Ceridwen Thomas in Standard I, died of croup. There was still no pure water at the school, but temperance teaching was given one period in the time-table, thus proving that officialdom had its priorities mixed.

Most of my memories of that school are happy ones, despite the fact that I was caned on the average three or four times a week. Caning was an old and accepted custom. Ovid[1] accused the morning of cheating boys of their sleep to deliver them to their masters who would inflict harsh strokes on their soft hands. The Headmaster was no better or worse than other headmasters of his day ; if your transgressed you were caned, and nearly always on the hands. If ' spare the rod and spoil the child ' had any truth in it we should all of us have been sprouting wings before the age of ten. The ration was two or three strokes on each hand. Many were the devices with which we experimented, to reduce the numbing pain of the strokes,—the hair of a horse's mane or tail so held between the fingers as to lie flat on the palm of the hand, was calculated to cause the cane to split and shiver. Alas ! it never did, although the legend persisted. Then there was the nice calculation of dropping

[1] *Amorum* 1.13.17.

the hand as the cane made contact,—this usually earned a bonus of two extra strokes. Girls were punished too, but were allotted one half the strokes awarded to boys—a constant cause of resentment with us. Punishment was carried out in the passage leading from the outdoor girls' yard to the big schoolroom, and on special occasions upstairs in a small attic reached via a steep staircase from the kindergarten room. I recall how one boy who was then thirteen became a hero to us all in an afternoon. He was awarded 6 strokes for a trivial offence, and he objected, with the result that the punishment was doubled. The Headmaster led the way up the stair as he had to unlock the door with a key, but Ben muttered, ' S'dim or diawl 'ma yn fy nghael i lan 'na ', ' This devil is not going to get me up there '. Foolishly the Headmaster tried to drag him up, but Ben successfully resisted by hooking his clogs between the pitchpine bannisters. Deadlock was reached. Thereupon the headmaster lost his self-control and like a maniac lay about Ben with the stick. It was a great mistake, for the lusty boy had now lost his temper too, and with one swipe sent his opponent's spectacles flying, and without them he could not see very well, and then there ensued a wrestling match which ended with Ben being the victor sitting astride the headmaster, and holding the latter's arms splayed out. He kept him thus, till he extracted a promise that he would never be beaten again, and this bargain was kept. But what a loss of dignity for a man in charge of a school ! During the war Ben became a Welsh Guardsman and won a splendid M.M. Having escaped death dozens of times in France, he came home to die, by awkwardly falling when hopping off a moving bus ! There were other characters in this school. One in particular was a fearless boy, Johnny, who pretended most realistically that he was a bird. At first he built nests in low trees by the road side—usually pollarded oaks with strong spreading branches. There he would sit, imitating all sorts of birds, and even sitting on a few addled goose eggs brought from home. But his passion for nesting grew, and he became a perfectionist, completely absorbed in his art. He now sought the tall trees. At a height of 60 feet and more, he would construct his great nests artistically, and with incredible skill. When he was a magpie for instance, he would weave withies in big loops to form a roof and a defence—but his star effort was the Giant Wren's nest—a huge structure with a roof and a hole for him to enter, through which he was able to disappear completely from sight inside it. The walls he made out of woven twigs cemented with clay and moss. We were as proud as Johnny was, of these gigantic nests which swayed with the wind in the high branches of most of the trees around the school. There was a profound psychological truth here—Johnny who felt inferior academically, was redressing the adverse balance by doing something he could do far better than anyone of us. One day he was scolded by the headmaster who said, 'Johnny don't be a fool—you are not a bird, and all these nests must come down, especially that big one you call the Wren's nest'. 'Never Sir', said Johnny, and off he ran to his refuge in the sky, which was swaying dangerously at the top of a huge conifer. The trial of strength was on, and afternoon lessons were at once doomed—for we all gathered around the tree. Johnny sulked out of sight inside his nest, and no one could induce him to emerge. At last, a School Manager, a highly respected bard and farmer—indeed he was a much better poet than farmer—arrived on the scene and shouted, 'Johnny come down will you, and give me a hand to get some of my cattle back—they have strayed into the churchyard and I'm afraid they will eat of the yew and die'. This produced a startling development—Johnny emerged and shouted, 'I'll be with you *mewn cachad*!'[1] and he slid outwards along a branch which bent with his weight thus enabling him to change in a rapid and continuous chain movement to a lower one, never hanging on one long enough to cause it to break, and so he slid safely down the outward tips of the branches. It was beautifully done, a kind of downward levitation performance, and we all yelled our spontaneous appreciation. There is no doubt that Johnny was a wayward genius, in so far as nature was concerned, and he was acclaimed as such by his fellow pupils.

He was also the first volunteer to be shot into space from a Roman catapult which we created. A very tall ash sapling was shorn of its branches except those forming a fork at its tip, and two laterals, which formed convenient foot rests. With the aid of a hay-cart rope pulled by 20 or more boys—this was bent down till Johnny could sit on the fork, and when he gave the word we let go—the objective being a terrace on the steeply rising ground which faced the tree. The slope was covered with black-thorn, gorse and brambles, and the bird-man's first flight ended in the midst of these. There were improvements made for the following day. Johnny who had gone back to the drawing board, arrived at school with huge wings made of sacking secured by binder twine to frames, but they did not

---

[1]i.e. Within the time it takes to defecate.

assist much either. Finally as the sapling became less elastic, we could roughly gauge where the likely landing would be, and after clearing a patch—even small boys were shot up. There was only one accident when a fellow named Titus made a bad landing, and cracked his ankle. Dear Johnny is still alive and working happily for a local farmer with whom he has made his home for years. He was no scholar—I doubt whether he ever learnt to write. If he were a schoolboy today our officious over-anxious bureaucrats would see to it that he went to a ' special ' school—that he was sent to a ' couch puncher ' and all to no purpose. The wiser way of the community into which he was born and brought up, saw to it, that he had a happy, useful normal life, to the mutual benefit of all concerned.

Another summer frolic was for three or four boys to climb young alders along the river bank. They were young because the Mills brothers had cut down the parent trees to make soles for clogs, and these young ones were suckers from the tods left behind. When they reached the top, the technique was to sway rhythmically till the point of no return was reached when the top snapped, and the lads came down with the leafy branchy top sometimes into the river, with their fall marvellously cushioned by the mass of branches and the green leaves full of sap.

But the greatest joy of the Summer term for Willie, Ianto and me, was to tickle trout in the neighbouring streams. We caught eels which were under stone slabs by a big quarry, and good sized trout as well. Where the water was deep we took off our shirts,—one never wore a vest, and two of us in turn held the third by the ankles, so that he could be immersed in the water and feel for the fish. Once a fish was located, it was imperative that it should not be frightened. Gently one hand was manoeuvred to enclose the head, and the other the tail. Steadily increasing pressure was exerted around the extremities of the fish, and the hands were pressed towards each other. It often helped if one could bring up some gravel with the fish, as this afforded a grip on the slimy creature. One of the biggest beatings we had was the result of putting several eels in the headmaster's desk. He did not consider it at all funny, for they had left stinking messes on his papers.

My most thrilling experience with eels took place on a Saturday morning in summer. I was going to the village shop a mile and a half away, and I was following the stream in the narrow valley, when I spotted a huge conger making its languid arrogant way to the deep mill pond 300 yards downstream. It was the largest I had ever seen, and I felt electrified. My scalp tingled at the sighting of this, to me, the most colossal creature of its kind I had ever seen, but how was I to catch it ? I ran down stream to where an old woollen factory building had collapsed partly into the stream. Here the river was wide and shallow, so I feverishly carried slabs of stone to build a causeway across the shallows. I lifted, with my newly-acquired strength, long fragments of lintels, which I placed as a dam across the stream, and over them the water was only an inch or two. Selecting a sharp-edged roof slate, and making no movement I waited in the path of this great eel. As its head came over the stone causeway I brought down this makeshift guillotine with all my strength, and then ensued a pandemonium of lashing and writhing, but the head was half-severed. Using both hands in an ecstasy of excitement, I scooped and tossed the wounded beast on to dry land—where I smashed its head with the aid of two stones. I carried it home on my shoulder, with its extremities touching the ground, skinned it and chopped its body into convenient lengths for frying. After a day in mild brine it provided several meals for the family, and nothing tasted more delicious than sections of this big eel fried in butter.

I believe that I fished almost as soon as I could walk. I used a bamboo stick with a gut line affixed to its top with a No. 4 or No. 5 hook, using lead shot to weigh it down. Red stripy worms from around the pigsties, were used as bait, and I fished clear or cloudy waters. There was one pool at the bottom of our garden, where a big trout lived, and my father and I both tried for weeks to lure him to our bait, but in vain. Then one day came heavy thunder rain, and I tried to tempt him again. He immediately took the worm, and then he was up in the garden. I was frightfully pleased and excited because I had beaten my father to it. Then as we boys grew older we used to club together in Summer and hire an old motor boat—a converted ship's lifeboat—and trawl for mackerel and pollock in the bay. To catch the first fish we used a piece of potato, sliced to resemble a minnow, and thereafter a piece of the shining belly of the first one caught. It was too easy ; mackerel are greedy indiscriminate feeders, just scavengers. It was not real fishing, but it meant a little pocket-money for us. We could sell most of them in the town, for a penny each, or seven for sixpence, and often at twelve for sixpence if the demand was small, because of rival catches competing.

Instruction at the school was efficient in a stilted kind of way, and within a rigid time-table. Welsh was neglected, just a token lesson or two a week. The damage this could have done was mitigated by the splendid teaching of Welsh in our Sunday School. Both my parents attended school when the *Welsh Not* was officially used to discourage a child from speaking its native tongue. This device was a piece of wood with a loop of string to hang it round the neck and a pupil with it could get rid of it only to another pupil who incautiously uttered a word of Welsh. The penalty of being caught with it was a severe beating. As late as 1852 Matthew Arnold, the Grand Cham of educational policy in Whitehall was prophesising with incredible arrogance that the Welsh language would be effaced, an event he described as socially and politically desirable.

But English was a favoured subject which had sub-divisions, almost complete subjects in themselves,—spelling, dictation, transcription, précis, composition, analysis. Geography meant memorising the bays, capes, rivers, mountains and cities of the country being studied, together with accounts of the peoples of many lands. History was unashamedly patriotic, full of jingoism,—after all, collectively were we not the finest, the bravest, the greatest ?

Dates had to be learnt for all the dynasties, and we had to distinguish the good rulers from the bad. Drawing was for boys only ; the girls took needlework. There was free-hand drawing with tremendous emphasis on shading, some geometrical objects to be drawn, for which a ruler was allowed. The greatest fun was painting with water colours, which had such intriguing names—burnt sienna, yellow ochre, vermillion or crimson lake. Calligraphy was considered important, but all we did was to copy the copperplate letters and words in the famous *copy-books*. Arithmetic was well-taught. Each week we had a test on the work covered—and there were innumerable sets of cards for use in class and at home, for of course we had homework in such an important subject. Music, too, was given several periods. We had to learn most of the patriotic songs of the United Kingdom, all of which were in Tonic Solfa, a system of notation which could be learnt after a few sessions with the modulator. Occasionally we had to transpose to and from the Old Notation, employing artificial aids such as *b a g f e d* or *f a c e* when the memory proved faulty. There was no opting out of any subject. Although I could read both Welsh and English at an early age, I was not quite at home speaking English till I was about seven or eight years old, for outside school, in the home or chapel it was all Welsh. Spelling came naturally, for I have a visual memory. A favourite piece of homework was to re-write in our own words, what we had read in class, or alternately to write a composition,—it never attained the dignity of an *Essay*, on a subject of the Headmaster's choosing.

My mother and her children were nurtured at the Board School on the *Royal Readers*, a series of six books brought out from 1872 onwards by Nelson, for use in schools. In these volumes there was a blended mixture of prose, poetry, illustrations, moral exhortations, uplifting examples of courage and sacrifice, useful knowledge—hints on sentence-making, arithmetical tables, geographical facts, history and biographical sketches, and lists of words with explanations of their difficulties. The prices were moderate, starting at 1½d. with the 64 page *Primer*, and rising to 2/0d. for the 446 pages of Book V. Mrs. Felicia Hemans, who at the early age of eight had written three verses, *On My Mother's Birthday*, figured largely in the volumes with her later poems. In Book I, as was logical, the children were given prayers to memorise for the morning, evening, and before meat. The quality of the poetry is pathetic,—for example—

> 'From Thy hand cometh every good ;
> We thank thee for our daily food ;
> O with it, Lord, thy blessing give,
> And to thy glory may we live '.

Nevertheless this prayer was more intelligible to the children than the gabbled Latin graces, of nobler and older institutions. Broadly speaking the children were taught that God saved,—the Devil destroyed. The description of the *Storm* ends,—' And at last all the poor men are saved. Kneel down, men, and thank God, who has saved you in the storm '. Mother was fond of reciting poetry to us, and we wondered where she had read them in the first instance so as to memorise them. They were all in the Royal Readers, and here is a selection of her favourites,—*Casabianca ; The Wreck of the Hesperus ; The Wind in a Frolic ; The Inchcape Bell ; The Burial of Sir John Moore ; He never smiled again*,—a reference to Henry I after the loss of his son Prince William who went down with the White Ship, *John Gilpin ; Bruce and the Spider ; The Deserted Village* and Thomas Hood's *The House where I was born.* I do not recollect her ever reciting a piece of Shakespeare to us, although the Royal Readers had several excerpts. Longfellow she liked—rightly, for he was a very good poet, and he would have been satisfied with Mother's verve and dramatic intensity when reciting,—' Tell me not in mournful numbers, Life is but an empty dream ! ' and the defiant crescendo of the voice with ' Life is real ! Life is earnest ! And the grave is not its goal !—so absorbed we would all be, that it needed the last verse, ' Let us, then, be up and doing, with a heart for any fate ' to remind her that the tickle in her nose was the smell of something burning, milk perhaps, or meat being overdone. For an encore she would recite *Lucy Grey*, or, and I think this was her favourite poem,—

' I remember, I remember,
The house where I was born,
The little window where the sun
Came peeping in at morn :
He never came a wink too soon,
Nor brought too long a day,
But now, I often wish the night
Had borne my breath away '.

She was a haphazard cook, loathed all house work, and much preferred to be outside in the open air. Best of all, she loved an interminable discussion incapable of a conclusion conducted amid never-ending cups of tea. If the conversation was interesting and the company pleasing, she would gladly stay down all night, and not go to bed. In less harsh an environment, with more liberal education facilities, she could have done well in commerce or the professions.

I consider that the *Royal Readers* were for their time unsurpassed, although they made only slight concessions to youth. There has been a deplorable tendency in the last 30 years to keep the child away from difficulties. Too many failed-teachers have become inspectors with power to institute easy reading and working in all subjects. Every child is a shorn lamb, for whom all winds have to be tempered. It is the failures who get the V.I.P. treatment. In my day we took the hard stuff neat. School leaving was at fourteen. By that time the bright pupils would have reached standard 7 or X7. The Headmaster, who was styled C.M., i.e. certificated master, taught Standards 4, 5, 6, 7 and X7. A lady teacher not college trained—just naturally gifted, took Standards 1, 2 and 3. In the other room another lady likewise non-college trained took charge of all the age groups 4—7 or 8. There were no formal games, but the teachers followed unashamedly the Board of Education Book of Physical Exercises which was lavishly illustrated with sketches. There was a good deal of arms bend—behind neck, etc., and much play was made by the kindergarten with wooden hoops. We all felt it was a lot of silly rot—and some of the more hefty jokers would pretend to groan with pain or exertion, as they tried to touch their toes. I can still conjure up the beatific vision of the Headmaster turning his back to the assembly to show how easy it was to touch his toes. He always wore green cycling knickerbockers—with a double seat sewn on. As he bent down his jacket fell over his head—exposing his braces stretched to the limit, and also his mighty bottom like a prehistoric mound. I devoutly hoped the leathers of his braces would sever the buttons. I could see it all—the subsequent giggling, the embarrassment of one looking silly, the final indiscriminate lashing out with the cane. Alas ! the leather moorings held fast, and we reluctantly allowed our pent-up breaths to escape in a subdued hiss full of regret, but feeling that we might be lucky next time a demonstration was provided. We did not have much, if any affection for the Headmaster, but we thought that the young lady teaching Standards 1, 2 and 3 was wonderful. I was later at the University with her younger brother who was 2 years my senior. He took a respectable degree in Chemistry, but then fell ill of T.B. and had to go home. The night he died, I had a vivid dream, in which he came to say goodbye with his hand outstretched, and as I was about to take his hand he vanished, and I woke up. I put on the light and noted the time. In the morning I narrated to my friends what I had experienced in the night, and when I came back at lunch time a telegram awaited me with the news he had died at the exact time of my dream. I do not try to explain it, apart from telepathy, which does exist between close friends, but there it is. His sister took to religion and would go down in dinner-break to the adjoining dingle and pray passionately. She too died prematurely, but she was a sweet woman, on whom Sir Lancelot would muse and say,—

‘ She has a lovely face ; God in His mercy lend her grace ’.

Clogs were the universal wear of all children during the week but on Sundays boots were worn—not shoes—but good solid leather boots with stout leather laces usually with the hold-fast mark, a sheet-bend, on each one.

A well-broken-in pair of clogs were comfortable, dry, and adapted to many uses but first of all let's start with the making of a clog. The sole was of sycamore or alder wood,—the latter was not considered to be as good, but it was sold commercially. As boys we often met along the banks of the stream the Mills team of fellers and shapers of the first stage of the soles. They camped in tents, improvised a low work block and set to work. We were fascinated by the speed with which they turned out pairs of matched soles, all done by the huge knife anchored to the block of wood. These they stacked to dry in what appeared to be giant circular bee-hives. I think that this was the first mass-production of clogs, and it may have been Cash & Co., who bought them and put the finishing touches on them. They were sold in their shops at less than our own clog-maker could afford to charge, but then they did not last so long. It was a great thrill to go the the workshop of Tommy our clogmaker. First he would measure with a sliding rule each foot, for he never failed to remark that no two feet were identical in size or shape. Then came the standing bare footed, on a piece of paper —while he drew the outline of each. The thickness of our stockings he allowed for—and they were quite thick being knitted of good stout, usually, grey wool. After this he measured what he called the height of the foot, that is, from the heel to the top of the instep. Then the time to collect and the price would be agreed, usually the next market day and four to ten shillings according to size. The great point for us boys was to ensure that the clogs had a tongue called water-proof—being sewn right up to the top of the uppers, and having a twin fold in it to expand sufficiently for the foot to enter. When new these folds could be painful, in fact a new pair of clogs coming up above the tender ankle bone was a tribulation we suffered patiently knowing that after the formative and breaking-in process, we should have a warm dry all-purpose footwear. The heels were shod with iron shoes and the soles with long races round the edges. The toe-cap had a brass band to protect the wood. Come the frost what excellent skates they were, and in the wet our feet were dry all day. Packed snow stuck to the soles of clogs making the wearer taller. There was keen rivalry to carry the tallest runcible lump of snow under one's foot. Another harmless prank was to establish the solid snow foundation, then walk across a brook without getting wet feet. Clogs were splendid football boots, but the only football we ever had was an inflated pig's bladder whose trajector on being slammed by a clog, was extremely erratic. Ultimately the day came when the sole cracked in two, usually as a result of jumping from the top of a wall onto the hard surface of the road, or when one landed after a summersault in the urinal stalls—when the landing was hard and noisy. A broken sole was a rare instrument for pinching the sole of the foot and a sheet of paper was immediately inserted to insulate against the jagged jaws of the fractured sole. Back again to Tommy, who would use the leather uppers, now moulded to all the contours of the human foot and for a few shillings one had another pair of clogs—but unlike the new pair these had already come to terms with the struggle against the protuberances of heel and ankle bones. Clogs had one unpleasant tendency—they caused stockings to wear into holes in the heels and many a sore was the result, often as big as half-crowns. There was no such thing as sticking-plaster in the first-aid outfit, only strips of clean white cloth cut from an old apron, and a jar of goose-grease. Later an ointment called Zam-Buk came in and created confidence in its use by its strong disinfectant smell. We always used the old goose-grease, and darned the torn stocking, a chore which we could all do after a fashion. These long black or grey woollen stockings came above the knee, with elastic garters to keep them up. No underpants or vests were worn with a flannelette shirt in summer, and a locally woven woollen one in winter. Refinements like cardigans or pull-overs were unknown, instead we had strong well-lined waistcoats, with four pockets. Buttons were sewn with waxed hempen thread, and no jacket had fewer than four buttons. Heavy gallaces kept up our trousers.

In families with half a dozen or so children to be clothed, there was a good deal of making-do by handing down the garments of the bigger to the next in line, size, or need. A boy might come to school on a Monday in the trousers and coat his brother wore the previous Friday. Mothers became resourceful in patching and cutting garments to size. The more adventurous would create suits for their sons, and dresses for their daughters. But the key man of the family with a clothes problem, was the itinerant tailor,—' Yr hen Deilwr Shonc ', a splendid old character, whose arrival was eagerly looked forward to, whose departure left a gap in the family circle whom he had regaled daily with wit and anecdote for a week or more. The date when you could expect to see him walking into your house was heavily underlined in *Old Moore's Almanack*, and was as important as any of the Saints' Days. We all had to take our places in the queue for his services. On average he came about twice a year. In addition to his superb technical skill, he had an inexhaustible stock of tasty, often salacious gossip. He knew who was prospering who was in trouble over rent, over illegitimate babies on the way and so forth. And he could imitate all the known preachers—their voices, mannerisms, and even the attitudes they struck. In fact at least two if not three of his own sons became Baptist preachers of the Word—and I remember them in top hats and frock coats. He certainly begat a talented family. I also remember one of his nephews, who was an undergraduate in my day, who became a distinguished scientist, starting his career with a top first in Chemistry. To return to our Tailor. He would begin by having a conference with our mother to decide what was needed. Then all the possible bits and pieces of raw materials would be laid out and allocated. First would come the patching so that garments already fit for relegation could be impressed into a few more months of service. Then came the planning and the designing of new garments which he would make. A cast-off Sunday suit of my father's would be dismantled and reassembled for my elder brother—how we envied him ! Then he might open his bag and display a man's corduroy trousers washed almost white—and this would do for us—we smaller boys. There was always beer when the Tailor was with us, and lots of delicious cawl—meat broth with all sorts of vegetables in it—a kind of superlative *minestrone*. He lived near enough to us to be able to go home to sleep—but if he worked on a distant farm he would sleep there, and of course there were no charges made for either board or lodging. God help him if he lived today—he would have been protected by Socialism and bureaucracy till he felt like a cocoon. Here was a free man who worked when he wished, and was happy and dispensed good cheer with his gossipy understanding and friendliness. He had a daughter who was a widow with three children, and she bought one of the early stocking knitting machines. With this she made new stockings, and also re-footed old ones, for stockings did not wear out above the ankles. You supplied your own wool and she would charge a very modest fee for her work. Life was hard in those days for most, but it had a satisfaction which bureaucracy has destroyed. There was a good deal of mutual help—a year's credit was usual and acceptable. We were all poor together, hence there was a magnificent communal spirit. Country folk everywhere can read the signs which indicate that things are not well—and very soon they know exactly what has gone wrong. Sometimes a sudden illness of the husband would make it difficult to do all the necessary chores. The word went round and the neighbours would share the work out between them, establishing a kind of roster. When my father was so dreadfully ill in bed upstairs, with rheumatic fever the neighbours came and cheerfully cut a hole through the bedroom floor—larger than the bed, then lowered the bed with father in it to the room below, *y parlwr* where there was a fireplace, a wicker armchair and a bed—the so called guest-bed with a starched valence all around it to hide the chamber-pots. The guest-bed was dismantled, taken upstairs and the joists and boards replaced. It was a great comfort to know that one had such loyal helpful neighbours. We met this feeling again during the last war when we were fighting alone against the forces of evil. The coming of victory and of prosperity has vitiated this spirit—one could almost say ' stained the white radiance of eternity '. Verily, poverty, too, has its compensations.

Lavatory facilities at the school were primitive to a degree. Water supplies were haphazard and depended on the vagaries and whims of a well, fitted with a hand pump. There was one tap for all the boys, and another for the girls. When the stench of urinal stalls became almost unbearable the cleaner would take some creosote to deal with it. Staff had one lavatory for ladies, and one for the Headmaster and male visitors. Both were identical and neither a masterpiece. A round hole in a seat of wood. Three feet below was a steep slope of concrete ending in an open cesspit. There was a terrible scene when one of the big boys, over-endowed with bucolic humour, gathered a huge posy of stinging nettles, and waited till one of the lady members of staff went to take her ease in this primitive privy. The reception which her tender bottom received, was stinging and shockingly startling, so she reported it to the Headmaster. No one, certainly not the culprit would confess—so he thrashed a boy whom he guessed might have done it. He lived to rue this for his victim waited with a bush of prickly holly for him in his turn to sit upon the seat with the bigger hole in it, and this lad having secured his line of retreat by opening one of the two halves of the double gate, was away in a flash down into the dingle, whose paths were as well known to him and the rest of the boys, as forest trails were to Red Indians. There is no doubt that the lesson went right home, and nothing more was said, only henceforth the gates leading to the cesspool were padlocked. We boys much preferred the freedom of the woods and the fields for our natural comfort, and instead of the local newspaper cut into squares, or the thin sheets of a G.W.R. time-table, we used green grass, or dock leaves. Sometimes half a dozen of us would take our ease in some corner of a field together, and I remember the different styles adopted. The boys of one family stood straight legged like giraffes, erect with legs apart, while performing Nature's behest, while others including myself squatted in great comfort on our haunches, thus making it possible to look backwards between our legs and notice how in summer the blue bottles were at their task before we had finished ours. There was a good deal of chat while sitting in such groups, and one noticed how some would join the club as it were, and go through the motions but with no success—just to be sociable. While on lavatory topics, the only game which had any connexion with it was that of playing fountains, to see who could hose his water the highest. The champion you would expect to be the boy with the tallest legs—but that strangely was not so. It was all in the preparation, so quarts of good clear water were drunk in the midday break from a well in a nearby field. Then with the full might of a distended bladder, victory could go to quite a dark horse. Everything was allowed,—the free-ranging sweep—the nonchalant climb higher and yet higher, till ceiling was reached, and the well-judged quick releases in jerks controlled by the finger and thumb. As far as I know not one of us came to any internal harm by sustaining such high bladder pressures.

Perhaps the greatest fun of any winter game was the terrific slide which we prepared in the steep fields below the school. I imagine the winters of my childhood were considerably colder than they now are, and a frost with all the bitter chill of a St. Agnes's Eve, would last several weeks. Many generations of school children enjoyed our well-prepared and exciting Cresta run, which must have extended five-hundred yards from start to finish. The owner of the field was Jonathan George, a School Manager, who always turned a blind eye to what was going on in it every winter. The beginning was a prepared run, down a 40° slope, then a short level section, followed by a very long steep slope, and on to the ice covered stretch to the river bank. The experts would get up such a speed, that they would shoot over the river where it was narrowest. Some natural springs fed the stretch next to the river, but we carried water up to the steep bits, and every morning it was frozen hard. I do not remember any one using a toboggan ; we all sat astride a cock-horse made of a piece of wood with its foot curved and shaped like a bando stick. Steering was effected by the use of the iron runners on our clogs. I am sure that there was not a more exciting experience than one's first attempt at this run. Once committed you were alone—so much alone that you heard nothing —saw nothing, till, if you had survived so far, you saw the yawning chasm of the river bed—also frozen—and then the final moment of truth—when with luck you would shoot off the high bank and land still in control, at least that was the theory of it, on the farther lower side, and come maybe to a graceful halt, but always a grateful one.

The biggest mass activity in which I ever took part, was the re-enactment of the battle of Hastings. We all made our own weapons, which included shields made of corrugated tin on a wooden frames, huge war axes of wood, terrific helmets which had begun life unexcitingly as farm buckets, and dozens of bows and arrows. We had to bring the weapons to the school secretly, hiding them in the hedges and in the dense dingles nearby. The Staff had no inkling of what we were planning to do, and unlike the set-up in modern wars, we had no informers in our midst. We all hid within easy reach of the school, till the teachers had gone home, and then the senior boys set the scene. There was only a handful of girls, and they huddled together by a clump of bushes. The Saxons occupied a small mound, with the Normans assembled down below. The two marshalls, one Norman, and one Saxon addressed the opposing sides in defiantly abusive terms. Duke William then gave a pep-talk to his men to the accompaniment of jeers and catcalls of the Saxons. Then it was Harold's turn, after which battle was joined and,

‘ So all day long the noise of battle roll'd
Among the mountains by the winter sea ’ ;

We Saxons knew that on this day, we could reverse the verdict of history. Before the archers had begun to empty their quivers, we had a splendid set-to with axes swords and spears. My friend Willie was a Norman. Full of guile he crept up on me, and while I was engaging another of his fellow-countrymen, he drove his spear at me. My shield partially parried the blow, lifting his weapon upward, with the net result that he broke one of my bottom left molars. Harold saw that the casualties were mounting rather too rapidly, so he gave us the order to charge—which we did, putting the Normans to headlong flight. Harold stayed behind on the mound fixing an arrow into his helmet, in a hole, previously prepared for this critical moment. We returned, and there was the prostrate leader, issuing his last commands. Poor Harold, he had no Excalibur, only a wooden sword made of slate batten. We therefore tidied ourselves, and wended our several ways to our homes. In the end the bruises and cuts told their tale, and we were forbidden ever to organise another activity of that kind. But how we enjoyed it, all of it, from the initial planning to the final execution. We were men for a while, and no adult present to say that we were only a bunch of crazy youngsters with an over-active sense of the histrionic, the historic, and the make-believe.

The alternative punishment to a caning, was detention after school, to write a specified number of lines composed of precepts smugly moral,—‘ I must not talk in class ’ ; ‘ I must always tell the truth ’ ; ‘ Honesty is its own reward ’. The work when done was to be handed to the cleaner when she came, or placed on the Headmaster's desk. Ingenuity became my downfall in the matter of lines, for at this time I had had more than my fair share of impositions. I decided to mass-produce these lines by constructing a wooden gadget which held 10 nibs, each of which touched the paper on the same plane. As soon as the Headmaster had gone, I assembled my contrivance and in no time at all, the completed lines were on his desk. Alas ! I rushed out only to find too late, that by an unlucky chance a local school manager had come that way, and was talking to the Headmaster half-way down the hill. There was no retreat, so I walked boldly past, doffed my cap, and waited for the storm to break in the morning. There was a dreadful scene—I was accused of cheating, of being dishonest, and so on, till I became angry and retorted that I had written the prescribed number of lines, and so what ? He said I could not have done them in the time, so with the pride of a youthful Michael Angelo I explained my invention. A reasonable man would have called it a day here, but no, my explanation incensed him the more, for I was now guilty of false pride as well as dishonesty, so he seized a thick cane and laid about me. All that day I brooded on the injustice which befall enterprising inventors who discover short cuts.

A regular check on attendance was made by a man named Phillips, who was called the *Whipper In.* He would ascertain from the register who was absent, and then he would visit their homes. Sometimes he found that children had been kept away from school, not by illness, but because of the birth of another baby, or to help with the harvest, in which case he would be understandingly mild, but unaccountable absences were stamped on severely. There was an obsession in those days with punctuality and attendance. Both boys and girls were caned on the hand for being only a few minutes late. It was barbaric, but accepted, for the belief was general, that without frequent application of the cane there would be no order, no progress in lessons, and no forming of character.

At school, fights were popular and frequent. My cousin Ianto, a month older, was a boy of great physical strength, and my ambition was to be able to beat him, but I never could although we often fought to a standstill. The students of form were active in arranging handicaps, for example, Ianto, Willie and I were in the Top League for our age-groups, so we would be matched against less lively gladiators with one hand each tied behind our backs. There was one nice strong boy whose technique was esoteric to a degree. On the signal being given to commence battle, he would about-turn, bend down, and with both arms acting as flails he would back, buttocks first against his opponent. He never realised how easily he could be sidestepped and given a bloody nose or a thick ear. There was also the popular attraction of matching three or more against five or seven less competent warriors. We three musketeers enjoyed this, and evolved a plan of moving in fast, deliver a couple of blows, and keep on moving—then when an opponent was discomfited or discouraged two of us would finish him off, and regroup swiftly with the third to further reduce the odds. Occasionally a hard-pressed boy would kick out, when the answer was to seize the foot and ankle, and swing him off his feet. If hard pressed one would stand back to back and slog it sternly out—waiting to see who'd last the longer. Perhaps that was why we loved to hear and recite Lars Porsena—no doubt, we were a sentimental lot—but life was good, for we felt that on the whole we dictated its terms. Willie and I were great friends from the age of four or five. As we lived so near each other we always did the journeys to and from school together. We would tag along, holding a red handkershief, but when bored by this, we would by mutual agreement decide to have a set-to. Farm servants watching us unobserved were startled at the ferocity of our fighting, but astounded to see it end, and we hand in hand trotting along again. It was our work-out and we felt we needed plenty of practice to stay at the top. The ' noble art of self defence ' attracted us strongly from an early age, so much so, that when we found a booklet about it with appropriate illustrations we experimented with all of them, counters, hooks, upper-cuts, in fact every trick in the book. We would never let anyone but Ianto persue this booklet, lest disaster befall us in the shape of someone who had done his homework more thoroughly than we had.

Nothing was too difficult for us to attempt—the magpie's nest high up at the top of a tall swaying tree, the teasing of bulls, which in those days ran free with the herds, with none of the modern practice of rationing sex, and armed with a hazel wand we would seize hold of the tails of bullocks, all for the sheer excitement of it. I recall how Joe the tall lanky son of the local farrier did not watch out for the high back kicks of a big beast, and appeared in afternoon school with a pair of lips larger than anyone could think possible, with a few teeth missing in the bargain. He was also the first boy in school to have his tonsils excised by a visiting doctor, whose chauffeur acted as anaesthetist being equipped with a sponge and a bottle of chloroform. There were no bounds to our admiration of Joe's father the Vet who, clad in leather coat and cap with fearsome goggles and leggings rode on a huge motor bike with epicyclic gears. We could only admire and worship real he-men. Saints on the whole rated pretty low. I felt it was difficult to become excited about St. David who did not appear to me to have done much. I was to learn better, years later, when an after-dinner speaker described how a Welsh International Rugger player when he died was received at the Golden Gates of Heaven. On being asked if he had anything to declare, he answered it was still on his conscience that the winning try he had scored against England, was from a forward pass, and he had never confessed to it while on earth. The saint patted him reassuringly saying, 'That was not a sin man—and don't call me St. Peter, I'm St. David and I'm standing in for St. Peter. You just go straight through '.

Gerald Cambrensis was much better, but the Navigator Prince Madoc, or Llewelyn our last Prince, or Owen Glendower—here were the heroes who really mattered. Of course, we were grateful to St. David for being the founder of our feast on 1st March. The parents would help with a splendid tea in the big classroom, then a stage was quickly erected, and prizes for the year's work presented. Then began the competitions with first, second and third prizes—1/-, 6d. and 3d. presented in a beautiful little silk bag with ribbon to hold it round the neck of the recipient. Girls would be asked to present prizes to the boys and vice-versa—all very pleasant, innocent and amusing. My father attended Llantood Board School, where on occasion the local farmers would supply the children with tea and cake. There was one teaparty in September 1897 which was described in the local newspaper, which added, that the liveliness of the scene was greatly intensified by the arrival of the Chairman of Llantood U.D. School Board, viz , Mr. Morris, Broyan, who with his exemplary generosity distributed two well filled hampers of buns among all the school children. Mr. Morris was a prosperous miller who could easily have spared the hungry children more than two hampers of buns ! On September 1897 when this feeding the multitude was being enacted in the Board Schools, Miss Haden who conducted a private school at 11 Pendre, Cardigan, was notifying the public that she had vacancies for Boarders. This year harvest ale cost 1½d. a pint.

Willie, Ianto and I were not averse to cutting other boys down to size. One day a new boy arrived who had been reared in industrial Wales, so he felt a good deal superior to all of us, and behaved accordingly. This was hard to stomach, but when he boasted that he could speak fluent Chinese, the three of us decided to call his bluff. We dangled him by his ankles over the parapet of the bridge, and threatened to drop him head first into the river unless he gave us a sample of his ability in this Oriental language. He was obviously scared, and a torrent of words poured from him, which he swore were Chinese. What he said was 'Gylm mah dee geista ; gulm mah dee geista ', repeated till we hauled him up. We were in a quandary, for we had never heard a word of Chinese, so giving him the benefit of the doubt, we warned him not to boast about it He didn't. Years later Ianto married his sister.

These, happily, were the days long before the 1944 Act which made a morning assembly and religious worship compulsory. What sort of religious service could we have had, for the majority of pupils were Baptists, and the Headmaster a Methodist. There was a handful of members of the Church of England, Dissenters and Methodists. There would have been dissention and accusations of not having a fair crack of the whip in regard to hymns, and of course the Baptists could not abide the Book of Common Prayer, and would have discovered Popery everywhere. The whole population would have been at each others throats, and no doubt the Baptists who had been so fervent and successful in dotting the fair land of South Wales with chapels, would have been equally fervent and successful in building their own schools for their offspring, staffed naturally by Baptist teachers trained at Baptist colleges. After all, the memory of *brad y llyfrau gleision*, the Betrayal of the Blue Books of 1847, was still fresh in the memory, and like seeping petrol any odd spark could ignite it. But enmity and discord disappeared from the district when death came. A Welsh funeral in those days was magnificent. I'm afraid the glory of this institution too is departing, with the growing practice of cremations, but what an uplifting experience it was for the bereaved family. When May John, one of my classmates, died of T.B. the whole school walked behind her coffin followed by the adults of the district. A simple service with a talk based on *Dyddiau dyn sydd fel glaswelltyn*, ' the days of man are as grass ', and the final sung *vale atque vale*, ' In the sweet bye and bye ' into which we put a good deal of feeling for, daily since her death we had rehearsed all that we had to sing.

The Welsh of my day faithfully attended every funeral in their district, and they were meticulous in their observance of the accepted ettiquette connected with the disposal of the dead. They followed a professional ritual. In the house of mourning for the husband or father who had departed this life, the bereft wife now a widow, would be accorded the privileges of a Queen of the May, except that she was dressed in black and wore no crown of flowers. She did no chores, but sat in sombre isolation while others brewed endless cups of tea, and passed around plates laden with cold ham, tongue, bread and butter and home-made cake. For those whose metabolism had received a shock, there was available in another part of the house, port, brandy or whisky. These mourners would arrive about an hour before the appointed time for the ceremony to begin. On reaching the threshold of the *salle d'attente* where the central character, the bereaved, was seated in state, Niobe all tears, in posture regal, the newly-arrived women mourners would be lined up. On the threshold they would momentarily halt to steady themselves, then take aim with moist beady eyes and waddle bent with bottoms out towards the stricken creature whose outstretched hand they grasped, while muttering inaudible comfort in her ear. This done each one was expertly guided to a seat to make room for others. The arrival of the minister was a signal for general but restrained weeping and wiping of eyes. The inexorable dénouement of the last rites called for sobs from the main character whose grief had to be both seen and heard. After the minister had read portions from the Old and the New Testaments, and offered up impromptu prayers meet for the occasion there would be a moment of silence followed by the sound of shuffling feet, and the odd bump or two to signify that the coffin had begun its last journey. The procession would form up outside and proceed to the burial place, passing *en route* houses with their blinds drawn. Buses, cars, carts, tractors, even ambulances would stop to allow the dead to take precedence over the living. After the service inside the chapel the coffin was then carried to the graveside and lowered, after which the orations began. I have heard as many as seven but this was unusual. These concluded, there would be the magnificent rendering of the final funeral hymn, and then the last prayer. The bereaved held firmly by the arms were led to the edge of the grave for a last misty look at the coffin. I recall being present at the funeral in Egypt of a British bank manager, and seeing one of his customers, a beautiful French lady, dropping a lovely bouquet on to his coffin and saying though her tears ' Bon voyage cheri '. Verily in the presence of death, flowers, even sprigs of acacia, can do nothing but bring comfort to the living.

I also remember the funeral of a poor old man who had once served in the Royal Navy—had seen much action in many climes, but afflicted by rheumatism, and a thirst greater than his capacity to pay, he was often in debt for small sums to various people. But when he came to settle his debt to his Maker, he was for a while the superior of us all—for high and low, rich and poor came to pay their last respects. It is still fresh in my memory, particularly that part of the oration with homely touches like ' Dai bâch thou has been in tight spots before, and thou art in one now, from which neither thy wit nor tears will release thee ; but the Great God who made thee, will not in His infinite mercy abandon thee now, and thou wilt arise clad in white, leaving behind thy old rheumatics and thy corrupt flesh—thou shalt wear immortality ; and be of the company of the saints, for the Lord thy God has forgiven thy trespasses,—Yes, Dai bâch, He has forgiven even thine '. This was good powerful medicine appreciated by all of us, and it was followed by the resurrection hymn with the immortal words by someone anonymous,—the last four lines of which were repeated several times,—

' Oll yn eu gynau gwynion,
Ac ar eu newydd wedd,
Yn debyg idd eu Harglwydd
Yn dod i'r lan o'r bedd '.

which toughly translated mean, ' All in their robes of white, transfigured, resembling their Lord, up-rising from the grave '.

The mourners like persons waking out of a trance would begin to take part, and as the melody weaved around the assembled gathering, its therapeutic effect could be detected in the straightening of the bent backs, and a renewal of confidence in their tear-washed faces, that all was well with him whom they had lost for a while, but would see again.

Another fine funeral hymn was Ieuan Glan Geirionydd's—

' Mae 'nghyfeillion adre'n myned
O fy mlaen o un i un '.

sung to the sad melody of the tune *Lausanne*. It is a soliloquy by the poet who sees his companions leaving him one by one to wear the crown and carry the palm. He imagines he can see them in fair Salem, and on occasions hear the echoes of their sweet singing. The time has almost come, when he too, will join them in that heavenly choir, with no more haunting fear of further farewells.

When a very old man died, his pals often older than he, would come to pay their last respects. Old Joseph who was a wag and approaching ninety, and an old gent who was ninety five were at the graveside of an old friend just as ancient. After the service Joseph, who was endowed with a sardonic wit, said, "Well Twm, I have been looking closely at you, and I should say it is hardly worth your while to go back home from here !"

Later these two were at another funeral in the same churchyard. As they were passing the grave of their old friend Twm said to

Joseph, ' We'll call on him on our way back '. A delightful thought which showed that to them he was not dead, only gone on ahead of them.

This same Joseph had a dog with a fine curly tail, a kind of Chow. One day he and his dog were in a cornfield, with the dog howling his head off. Our neighbour James asked him what the matter was with the dog—was he mad ? ' O, no ', said Joseph, ' he's just sitting with his bare bottom on a thistle, but he's too lazy to get up '.

The Welsh practice of eulogising the dead at their funerals would not have appealed to a very famous Baptist preacher the Rev. C. H. Spurgeon whose 1963 edition of *John Ploughman's Talk,* was the 560th thousand. It was one of mother's favourite books into which she dipped for wisecracks. Writing on Monuments Mr. Spurgeon asks, ' Where do they bury the bad people ? Right and left in our churchyard, they seem all to have been the best of folks, a regular nest of saints, and some of them so precious good, it is no wonder they died—they were too fine to live in such a wicked world as this. Better give bread to the poor than stones to the dead. Better kind words to the living than fine speeches over the grave. Some of the fulsome stuff on monuments is enough to make a dead man blush '. The old Welsh funeral of my yesterdays, was kind, dignified, forgiving, indulgent, humorous, comforting, helpful, a tacit acknowledgement of our frailty—of the inexorable, unavoidable debt we should all one day have to pay, we all owed God a death. So a Welsh crowd at a funeral shared an uplifting spiritual experience, and were all the better for having done so.

One of my earliest recollections of death was when my Grandfather James died. He was my Father's father, and on Sunday before the funeral all the relatives were gathered, and also friends of the family. He was lying in state in his coffin, across the window of the parlour. One by one, and in groups, the visitors were taken to have their last look at James. I followed them several times, but was too small to see into the coffin. When I begged someone to lift me up to see I was scooted out unceremoniously. Biding my time when there was a lull for tea, I sneaked in by myself, dragged a stool to the side of the coffin and had a good look. I remember how very cold his forehead was, and that his flesh was hard, like the chaps of a slaughtered pig. Apart from that I felt no great emotion. As a family our attitude to death has always been practical. Mother made us promise that we should not buy black suits, ties, overcoats, or any other kind of dark mourning for her funeral, and I attended her funeral in my favourite green suit of Welsh flannel. Other members of the family donned what they felt was their best suit, not one of which was black.

The cost of dying in the country parts of Wales would appear most reasonable by today's standards, but not so reasonable when it is remembered that a farm labourer earned on average less than 9/6 a week with no scheduled hours or overtime pay. Most labourers would have a small holding of five to seven acres, which the wife would manage with the aid of her children and occasionally her husband when he could obtain time off.

My Grandmother—mother's mother died on 9 January 1893, the cause of death being noted as 'Failure of Heart from debility'. Her age was 40, so debility could cover a multiplicity of fatal causes, ranging from slow starvation to T.B. I have the receipted bill for her coffin,—To Wm Lewis Carpenter Penybryn. Jan'y 11th 1893.

To Coffin for the body of the late Anne Thomas

To Coffin & lining	2 ,, 12 ,, 0
Shroud	0 ,, 6 ,, 0
	2 ,, 18 ,, 0

Settled the above

Jan'y 11th 1893

Wm Lewis [across a Penny Queen Victoria stamp]

Apart from the basic cost of the actual coffin and shroud, a family funeral meant new black Welsh flannel overcoats. In 1905 on the death of Grandfather James, Owen Evans and Sons charged £10 for five, one each for us three children, and the other two for our parents. This appears to have been a high price for the same tailor charged 12/- for a pair of breeches, which by today's standard was exceptional value. The laying out of money was an art which mother seems to have learnt at a very early age, especially with babies regularly on the way—and all the tasks connected with the holding to be discharged wet or fine, winter and summer. What a splendid manager she was ! On Feb. 19, 1904 she paid John Lewis Forge Cych Factory the following :

10½ lbs White Yarn	4	3	6
13½ yard Carsy Flannel	5	5	7½
9½ gray yarn	4	3	2
4½ Blue colour wool	8	3	0
8½ yard Flannel shurt	3½	2	5½
6½ yard stripe Flannel Petty	4½	2	3

12 yard weaving Blanket			8	6
5 yard Petty	3		1	3
13½ yard Black colour gown			5	6
pair Blanket			3	4
		1	18	7

Settled John Lewis
April 23 1904

Mother was born on 18 June 1875, so she was left an orphan when she was seventeen and a half years of age. On the 11 November 1893 when they were both 18 my father married her, and in March 1895 my brother Jack the first of six children arrived.

Carsy of course is the Suffolk Kersey. On the bill head Mr. Lewis states his trading terms, Accounts Quarterly. Interest charged on overdue Accounts. From what I have been able to gather, Mr. Lewis never charged interest on any overdue accounts. He knew, full well, the particular reason for failing to pay by a given date. Another item was heating—and although wood was extensively used as fuel, there was a wretched kind of grate between the brick oven and the open corner fire with its tripod hooks and chain for the big boilers. This range had an open fire between its oven and a boiler which in theory held clean hot water, but it was never better than a smelling mass of rusty water which was used to mix with the pig meal. This open fire was of culm-balls, a fuel now almost unknown. In March 1895 Father paid 9/7½ for 15 ct 2 qrs culm at 7d per ct. delivered by the local carrier whose wife and daughter conducted the village shop. The bill was paid in February 1896. In July 1909 the 7d grade culm was still available with a better grade at 10d a cwt. and father at that date had 19 cwts of each and mixed them. He paid for them on 24 August 1910, and the merchant, James Adams & Co, Coal, Lime, Manure, Seed & Butter Merchants had now a new bill head which stated ' Terms—Cash '. On 5 Sept. 1910 Father paid for the old 7d culm at the rate of 8½d and it arrived on 5 October, by John James's cart. It is clear that there was hardly any inflation at this time. A word or two further about culm. It was coal dust and the poorer the grade the less heat it gave out and the less it lasted. Culm balls were prepared in this way. Clay which we dug up, the bluer the better, was dried in the sun to begin with and then under cover. It was pounded by a ram, that is, a heavy wood pestle—to a fine grading, and mixed, I think in a one to seven proportion with the culm. This was then thoroughly mixed with water, until it was of a ' gooey ' consistence, and a heap was always ready in the outhouse. A bucketful of this always stood near the fire and with the occasional addition of a little water, the balls were made and the fire raked of its ashes and rebuilt with fresh culm balls. It was quite an art. If the fire was not urgently needed it was sealed with a top slab of culm with one or two vent holes made with the long iron poker. Through this hole escaped the burning carbon monoxide. It was at it best only a passable fire, its only real virtue being its ability to keep alight all night, and if one went out for a lengthy period, a series of vigorous pokes and up it came to boil a kettle or heat a frying pan. Wood fires had to be constantly fed—but how much more comforting they were. Mother always baked in a big oven heated by billets of oak, ash, or sycamore, with the occasional old apple tree. Ash was a splendid burner, green or dry, but oak steadied the temperature. The juice of green ash as it burnt was a specific for ear ache. I do not remember burning elm which is excellent fuel wood, used by the Romans to fire their kilns, but the reason was the scarcity of elms whereas the other woods were plentiful. In all my travels I have never tasted either bread or butter to equal those my mother made not even the fresh French *baguette* with Breton *demi-sel* spread on it. The average loaf was anything from 18 inches to 2 feet in diameter. Enough bread would be baked to last the household a week at least. She baked pure white Spillers ' As You Like It ' flour, and also mixed oatmeal and barley flour, so there would be three kinds of bread from which to choose. Large slices of this bread with all the air pockets filled with the salted butter—and the cawl with meat and vegetables in it, composed a meal fit for royalty. God knows what is extracted from the flour today before it is used by the multiple steam bakers to make what we should refuse to eat, if only we cared for food as the French do. As Wordsworth said in 1802, England is still at times ' a fen of stagnant waters '. Only a minority care enough about food standards, to protest violently when they fail to satisfy. The personal touch has now been lost, and the integrity of flour vanished. In my childhood we took the oats, the wheat and the barley to the local mill, and after discussion with the miller, we arrived at the exact kind of fineness best suited to our taste, and the exact amount of husk, if any, to be left in the final product. The cast-iron floor of our old brick oven had a hole in it about half an inch or more in diameter. This allowed the dough to sink into it with the result that every loaf had a beautiful well browned nipple, which would not have been amiss on Messalina when she went topless. We all wanted this, when a new loaf was being cut, and the first one to stake a claim usually got it. It was well-cooked, well-browned, crusty and chewy.

We also believed that a good deal of what we fancied did us good. Willie has more than once told me about his father Joseph, who liked nothing better than large slices of fat home-cured bacon fried with eggs, or boiled with potatoes and other vegetables when in season. His doctor called during a 'flu epidemic, and on running the rule over him, was horrified at his blood pressure and at once prescribed a strict diet, together with a total ban on the consumption of fat bacon. Joseph listened most courteously, but when the medical man had departed, he ate a substantial meal composed mainly of fat bacon. Years later Willie reminded his father of the doctor's advice and suggested he should try it for a while. The reply was typical, ' Where now is the young doctor who gave me that advice ? he is dead, but I am still alive and well, enjoying my fat Welsh bacon ! ' And without changing his eating habits he went on to live till he was nearly ninety, when he died of pneumonia following the fracture of a femur when he slipped and fell on the icy farmyard.

Professional men lived on farms and in his early married life my father worked at 9/6 a week, for our local doctor, James Mathias Phillips, M.A., M.D., C.M., M.R.C.S., J.P., whose son, also a doctor I met in the twenties in Cairo, where he was Professor at Kasr el Aini Hospital. The bill Dr. Phillips presented for professional attendance upon my father including medicine in 1901 when he was ill with typhoid came to £2-19-2. He visited on horseback during the period 12 February to 4 March. Throughout that time mother slept with my father, but no one else contracted the disease, for she carried out most scrupulously, the advice of this wise old medic—to isolate everything my father used—wash everything in boiling water—and not put any fingers or hands in mouth, for as he explained, the disease was contagious but not infectious. Dr. Phillips died on 14 April 1903 at the age of 64, having practised medicine for 30 years. Local solicitors who had their offices in the town would live on farms a convenient distance away, and one of them, a charming man who was a friend of our family had a farm next door, and no one excelled him as a judge of land and stock. He would walk over a farm on behalf of a client, and there and then he would estimate its value, and he was never proved out in his valuation.

PATCH-WORK QUILTS

My mother had a passion for patchwork quilts, a species of hoarding, or perhaps a collector's mania. Every spare drawer or coffer in the house would be squeezed tight with these exquisite creations, made by an elderly widow and her daughter who was somewhat ' simple '. But with the traditional custom of the family looking after its own, she more than earned her keep. They have been dead now for many years, and their cottage and garden have been supplanted by a ' slazy ' bungalow with no garden, for the modern trend is to regard a garden as a liability. When there was no more room in our house for quilts, mother would give them away. They were of two kinds, the light-weight and the heavy. We liked the heavy ones ; their weight was a comfort as we snuggled underneath them in winter, when the frost sparkled like myriads of diamonds on the slates visible inside the bedroom for there was no ceiling. We never slept on sheets—they were only for guests—but between a pair of Welsh woollen blankets—on top of which we might have four or five quilts. Like all children we were naughty, and these sturdy quilts were pressed into service sometimes as tents, and when we were reading naval yarns—Hurricane Hurry was a favourite—we used to tie each end with a strong cord, and sling them between the two oak trusses which were secured to the oak crucks by stout pegs. Sometimes a hammock was slung between the two purlins, which again, were whole oaks sawn down the middle. General horse-play and fooling around often resulted in a foot going through, and the quilts would then have to go back for repairs. On sunny hazeling days we used to help Mother to carry the quilts out into the sunshine on to the clean grass in the orchard where they were spread. Some of them had large panels made up of many patches, and we always felt that our reward for helping was to get mother to give us the story of each patch. I'm sure she invented some of the answers—for they were not always the same, but to us they were an evergreen saga,—'That's Auntie Mary's first frock—and that a piece of my wedding dress ; Ah ! Yes, those three, pointing to newish looking patches, were remnants I bought at the Cloth Hall, after I sold our first four porkers, and those were also remnants of a faded piece I bought cheap at the Bon Marché. Her masterpiece was left to the last,—when she would modulate her voice into one suitable to the solemnity of the occasion, ' And this, was a piece left out from the shroud of your Grandfather. William Lewis (the undertaker) gave it to me, and said I'd be sure to find a use for it ! ' I have often wondered who designed the wonderfully intricate patterns of the quilting. The old ladies who quilted, had them in their heads, and never hesitated—it was like superimposing in exquisite needlework the elaborate scrolls of wrought iron, the only straight lines being those that framed the quilt along its edges. Mother supplied the materials, and we sometimes helped to wash and teazel the wool, which was the meat of the sandwich, the amount of which was varied according to the thickness and weight required. Nearly all the wool was gathered from bushes, brambles and barbed-wire under which sheep had passed leaving behind parts of their fleece. An old woman who came to buy eggs called Maria the Eggs, would often bring a contribution of wool gathered as she wended through the fields from one farm to another.

Wool-gathering of another kind was my favourite form of escapism when the lesson in progress was dull. A sharp rap on the knuckles was the method adopted by a teacher to bring one back to reality, an abrupt termination to the magic journeyings of the mind. The duller a teacher was the more he resented any attempt to escape by one of his captive audience.

Potential quilt patches were kept in a clean meal bag which had been washed several times, while another bag contained the wool. There was yet another sack with fascinating contents,—the bits and pieces that were to be used for patching our clothes, a hotchpotch of dresses, underwear, shirts,—woollen and flannelette, corduroys, heavy overcoats, and a coachman's cape. When we had nothing else to do, we often emptied this bag and occasionally dressed up in garments far too big for us. Once so dressed, we would be any character from Jack the Ripper to the Angel Gabriel complete with goose wings borrowed from downstairs. Finally, by way of treasure trove, there were two or three tin tea caddies filled with all kinds of buttons and buckles. We particularly enjoyed the military ones, and I remember sewing one or two on to the fly of my trousers. I'm sure that anyone seeing me proudly showing off these buttons would have immediately jumped to the conclusion that I was addicted to indecent exposure ! There was also a pair of brass buckles which were once part of a naval officer's belt. I restored it, and wore it proudly for several years. We could never get mother to tell us where it came from. She said it had always been in the house, and that her grandfather had it. Whoever had originally owned it, he would have been quite happy with the brave roles assigned to him in our many charades. He was never defenceless, for on these occasions a cutlass, provenance unknown, was always stuck in his famous belt.

THE FLYING COFFIN

I remember, still with a sense of awful glee, the case of the flying coffin. This was not an epic in the tradition of Dan McGrew, but something in which I inadvertently participated. It was in the winter of 1916/17 and the War was going badly, but Benchi the jovial Welsh Guardsman was home on his first leave from the trenches in France. Death had stalked him hitherto in vain, all it had to its credit was a notch in his right ear, but his eyes had become accustomed to the sight of dead men, and his nose could endure the stink of corruption. His father and his grandfather had been the local carpenters and undertakers, and the business was now carried on by the eldest son William, who by upbringing and the nature of his calling was inclined to be serious and religious-minded. Not so, Benchi, a born practical joker, who, since he had been with the Welsh Guards, had learnt some extraordinary songs, which he sang in his beautiful tenor voice, radiating the authentic spirit of the old buccaneers, or the risqué ditties sung by Daudet's monk after repeated tastings of the heavenly elixir he was brewing. But not a pleasant fellow for a Jerry to meet in no-man's land.

The tale of the flying coffin would never have been told, had not something dreadful happened almost as soon as he had arrived home on leave. In an almost inaccessible cottage high up in our valley lived a poor, bearded loud-mouthed peasant, who frequently took aboard too much liquor, after which he quarrelled violently with everybody including his wife and children. The eldest boy, although only fifteen, took the side of his mother. The father eked out a living by hauling with his horse and cart, but the heavy snow had made this impossible for over two weeks, and so he had ample leisure to abuse his wife. The climax was reached when he roared into the house, brandishing a butcher's knife. The mother called on her son for help and the outcome was that in the ensuing struggle he fell onto the knife, and expired. The doctor was called and he performed the post-mortem in the outhouse. At the Coroner's inquest the verdict of death by misadventure was returned, the family receiving much sympathy, and an assurance that they were in no way to blame, as indeed, they were not.

The next natural step was to order a coffin in oak, for in those days no other wood was considered decent enough to house the dear departed, and I recall as if it were yesterday how William and Benchi with a younger brother asked me to guide and help them over the snow, through the woods to the isolated croft in the *cwm*. A pony cart was used to transport us and the coffin as far as an adjoining big farm, but the ground was impassable from there on, so we manhandled our load over three fields, till we could see our destination—the small house nestling at the foot of the steep side of the narrow valley. It was full moon and the deep snow was frozen solid. We deposited the coffin on top of the ride which resembled nothing more than an Olympic ski run. William removed the lid to get at his bag of tools, and also the webbing which he was going to attach to the coffin for safety sake, while we were transporting it down the zig-zag sledge-track now completely obliterated by the heavy fall of snow. Whether it was intentional or not, I shall never be able to decide, but Benchi who was at the front end suddenly shouted to me,—' Jump in, the darn thing is on the move '. It was, and all I could do was to grasp frantically at the stern of the flying ark. William and his younger brother were quickly left far behind with the lid and the bag of tools. It was lucky that I had not been able to jump aboard as Benchi had done, for I had become by no wish of my own, the helmsman. The technique was well-known to us, and as I was wearing clogs I raked with the tenuous confidence born of necessity but the breath-taking speed, the insane exhilaration, and the feeling that we were participating in something akin to black mass were also present. Benchi had recovered his composure and was there sitting amidships in our unorthodox conveyance, shouting directions to me. At the rate we were travelling we were not going to stop till we reached the outhouse where the body lay, and to do this we had to negotiate first, a gap of about 4 feet and a gate which we prayed would be open. The gap was coming up on us so fast that we had no time for idle thoughts. We flashed through with the sweat on my forehead cooling and numbing like an anaesthetic in the freezing air. Only one more hazard to negotiate, the sharpish bend to the outhouse. Benchi leaned inwards, while I hanged out the tail, and we drifted to a stop sideways against a cock of hay covered with snow. This put a harmless end to our breath-taking drop down a Welsh Cresta run.

The reaction was swift—hysterical laughter, and ribald remarks about the slowness of its next trip. It was over 20 minutes before the two brothers joined us. When they did all they could utter was 'Duwcs annwyl' 'Dear God. Dear God', until finally the grisly humour of the situation overwhelmed them both, and there was another outburst of hysterical laughter, in which we joined. This brought to the door the widow, to whom William went to say that he had come to transfer her late lamented into his cerecloth and so forth. 'Do what you like to him', she said, 'I don't want to see him, but when you finish come in to have a cup of tea'. We lit the hurricane lamp and began to load. The main difficulty was immediately apparent—*rigor mortis* had set in while the corpse was not laid out, and the knees were several inches above the gunnels when it was laid in the coffin. 'Dear God', said William, 'what do we do now. Good God! Good God!' Benchi supplied the answer saying he could do with the hot tea, and mounting on to the knees he bounced up and down when suddenly they collapsed and the bearded face of the dead man came right up to his. 'Damn it all man!' he said, 'I don't fancy your cold kisses', and then in a gentle voice full of compassion, he added as if addressing a little child, 'the time for making love is past, and you must now lie down'. With that he pressed the upper part of the torso down, and the lid was screwed on tight. Never, I vow, did tea and a piece of bread and butter taste so well. In Wales, Death is a comprehensive answer, and the old reprobate, the inveterate wife-beater was given a splendid funeral, with relays of bearers carrying him along the frozen tracks to his final resting place. Women are inexplicably wonderful—for his widow is on record as saying, 'I'd have him back tomorrow, there was no one quite like him',—and by God there wasn't.

KILLING THE PIG

One of the most important tasks of the year was to slaughter the fat pig, which weighed as a rule anything from 16 to 20 score live weight. It was not strictly speaking, a task, more of a ritual, a blood sacrifice. The carefully selected pig was well fed, from the time he was chosen for his high destiny till the moment of truth on a cold winter morning, when he was betrayed by those whom he thought were his friends. The final stages of his diet consisted of milk, potatoes, and plenty of barley meal. Any old crusts of bread, and scraps from the table were added as tit-bits. Like the victim chosen for human sacrifices in ancient times, nothing was too good for him. No processed fish-food was ever fed to him, as the fishy taste would persist after death in the meat. The pig's bed was plenty of clean straw, changed regularly, into which he would burrow and relax into a nourishing 'fattening' sleep. The ceremonial slaughter of the sleek beast would take place around Christmas, or the New Year, and always during a waxing moon, never when it waned. I was always informed by the local wise men, that the bacon from a pig slaughtered when the moon was 'on her weakness'[1] would not cure properly, and would be heir to most of the consequent blemishes, rancidity, mould, slime and even worse. On the day appointed the big brass pan would be placed on its tripod, with a huge log fire underneath to heat the water needed to dehair the animal. As soon as the 'pig-sticker', a prominent deacon and precentor with the Baptists, arrived with his satchel of tools, he would first of all have a tot of brandy with my father, always Hennessy with its tradesmark of an armoured arm with the hand clutching a medieval

---

[1]In Provence gardeners believe that beans and peas being amorous (clinging) must be sown during the moon's first quarter, but potatoes and root vegetables being phlegmatic, must be sown during the last quarter of the moon, as then she will pull down their roots as she sinks. All this, and more is enchantingly described by Lady Fortescue in her book, *Perfume From Provence.*

battle-axe. Then an inspection of the boiling water to ensure that it was coming up to around 150°F, and up to the pig-sty where the poor unsuspecting creature, having been starved of solids for 36 hours fondly believed that food was nigh, instead of which he had a line with a running noose and a half-hitch secured around his upper jaw.[1] He was propelled along quite slowly, a veritable mountain of meat, to the place in front of the doorway to the outhouse adjoining the house, the door of which lay on the ground ready to receive the victim. My father would hold the pig's head up with his line, and my job was to steady the animal by gripping the tail. The sticking knife was 8 to 9 inches long, and the point was razor sharp on both sides. Our butcher always shaved off the bristles in the sticking area, and it was pathetic to hear the pig's squeals changing into grunts of satisfaction as the shaving process soothingly tickled him. Then the knife was inserted at an angle of 45° to a depth of 6 inches, and the carotid and internal pectoral arteries severed. If the operation was properly carried out, the blood gushed out in a torrent, the eyes soon became glazed, and the animal subsided gently on to the door, oblivious that with his death, he had secured freedom from hunger for a whole family for the forthcoming twelve-month. This was the time to raise the back-quarters of the pig to give the blood a fall. Next came the hot water in tin jugs, and the bristles scraped off by sharp tin lids. In order to hoist the clean carcass it was dragged on to a ladder, the tendons of the hind legs being raised by cutting along the back of the leg, and a gambrel *cambren* pushed through. A double pulley lifted the carcass by the gambrel when it had been carried inside the outhouse on the ladder, and it hung head downward from an oak beam. A well-washed potato kept the mouth open, and a tub was placed underneath to catch any remnant of blood.

A long cut was now made from between the hind legs along the middle of the distended belly as far as the neck, care being taken not to pierce the caul or intestines, by inserting a finger on either side of the knife, and pressing inwards. When the rectum had been

[1]This was absolutely necessary as no self-respecting pig would allow himself, if free, to be killed without putting up a struggle. The beautiful illustration in BM. *Add. MS.* 24098, f. 29v where a maid is holding a frying-pan to catch the blood, while the butcher unassisted is holding the squealing pig on the ground and sticking it, can only be described as artist's licence.

cut around, the whole of the intestines and stomach fell naturally into a large pail or tub. The gall bladder was severed from the liver and set aside to be hung in the house and used to draw thorns out of one's hands ; it seems to have worked. The flare fat and the kidneys were left inside. The belly was kept wide open by a spreader, and having cut the joints of the fore-legs at the wrist, as it were, the pig-sticker was now free to wash, and take his ease over his tea of bacon, egg and heavy home-made fruit cake. Gossip was dispensed —the world put to rights, and in the dark, the man of blood with another Hennessy or two inside him departed on his cross-country journey home. Verily a dangerous man to accost or attack, armed as he was with a varied selection of sharp knives.

I always helped the next evening, when the flesh had cooled solid, to cut and trim the carcass. First the head was cut off close behind the ears, the back-bone removed with the tail attached, and a side at a time placed on an old table which had been scrubbed. The flare fat, kidneys, and ribs were removed and the whole side cut into three—ham, middle, and fore-leg. There were no sub-divisions into loin, belly, etc. Several dishes were heaped with choice fillet steaks which were not left to be cured as the strong salt would make them too salty. The pig's tail was chopped off, and put aside with the trotters, ears, pluck, tongue, brain, caul (we called it shawl), kidneys, all of which were used to make faggots, brawn, sausage and delectable puddings. The one part of a pig's offal which was always thrown away was the spleen *poten ludw* and I seem to remember that it was rejected also by both cat and dog—why I could not tell. The intestines altogether about sixty feet of them, were turned inside out and scraped, after which they were cut into lengths and cleansed in warm salt water. Some were chopped, mixed with pieces of stomach, and fried with onions. I never cared for the bitter taste of this dish. But there would be lots of roast ribs and fried steaks—which were delicious hot or cold. There was also the pleasing custom of taking a few choice pieces to our neighbours, who in their turn, would reciprocate, when they had killed their pig. The house smelled for days of roasting, frying, and baking, and the atmosphere was greasy from the never-ending rendering down into lard of the flare fat. We never used the bladder to contain lard, though many did, the hot liquid being poured into a tundish inserted in the neck of the bladder, a tricky domestic operation, as spilt molten lard inflicted nasty burns. So on each pig-killing occasion the bladder became a veritable treasure for us boys. It was blown up—the tube tied and then its length shortened, and it was proudly taken to school and used as a football. Its flight after being kicked was wholly unpredictable, thus adding to the interest of the game. It was incredibly tough, as of course it had to be, to withstand the constant lambasting from metal-tipped clogs. Disaster usually met it when after being kicked over the wall, it would land on a thorn bush and be punctured. We never learnt of a way to mend a punctured pig's bladder.

Meanwhile a reception was being prepared for the 6 main pieces of pig to which was added the chin, or jowl. A wooden vat called *noe* was lined with salt which we bought in 'bars' weighing 14 lbs. each, which we had to render into powder. The salt was well rubbed into the sides and hams which were placed skin downwards on the prepared bed of salt. After a day or two saltpetre was rubbed on the flesh—but not on the skin. Adding salt was continued for about 7 or 8 days, after which the vat contained a good deal of brine and the absorption of salt was now slow. The pieces were moved daily, but left for a total of about a month before they were lifted out, and hung to dry for a few days before being taken indoors to the big old-fashioned farm-house chimney, where they were strung up in serried ranks, being kept separate by bunches of holly. Mother claimed she could forecast the weather by examining the salt moisture on the sides of bacon. I was most interested while reading a pamphlet[1] on home-curing of bacon, to find quoted the curing recipe[2] of Cato the Censor, which he wrote in 200 B.C. Cato reported that in Lombardy three to four thousand sides were salted every year. Lombardy is still well-known for its ham, and various dishes made from pig meat and offal. In Modena or Bologna you can have an extensive choice of meat dishes based upon the pig. Cato describes the curing process 'When you have bought your hams, cut off the hoofs. Take half a peck of Roman salt ground fine for each. Lay salt over the bottom of the tub; then put in a ham, the skin side downwards. Cover it all with salt. Then put another ham on top, taking care that meat does not touch meat. So deal with them all. When you have them all in position put salt over them, so that no meat is visible and level off with salt. After five days take them all out and the salt with them.

---

[1]*Home Curing of Bacon and Hams. Bulletin No. 127 of the Ministry of Agriculture and Fisheries.* H.M. Stationery Office, 1943. This is a most excellent pamphlet.

[2]*De Agri Cultura* 162 which is the last section.

Put them in again so that those which were at the top are now at the bottom. Cover them over with salt as before. After a total of twelve days at most take the ham out, rub off all the salt, and hang them up in a draught for two days. On the third day wipe well all over with a sponge, and rub them with olive oil. Hang them for two days in the smoke. Take down, rub well with a mixture of oil and vinegar, and hang up in the meat store '. Except for the exclusion of olive oil this was the method of home curing generally in use in Wales. Did the ancient Welsh copy the recipe from the Romans ? One wonders.

The cottager's pig in my day was the mainstay of his domestic economy. Before we became so foolish and prudish about natural smells, every house in town and country had a pig sty in the garden. The pig ate any ' left-overs ' and there were cabbage leaves, potatoes, and acorns available to supplement his diet. His manure when its heat had slaked, was used to feed the garden soil. Hens were universally kept, and so were ducks if a pond or stream was accessible. A few healthy rabbits could always be poached, and a piece of belly bacon was mixed with rabbit to make a magnificent family pie.

Then there was the sad case of the Tamworth runt, which was presented to mother. Nothing absorbed her more than caring for the sick, the weak, or the maimed members of the animal kingdom. This was a comic little piglet with head almost the size of his body. He was nursed to begin with in a cardboard box lined with a Welsh wool blanket, placed on the hob. He was fed on milk by means of a Swan fountain pen filler, and he made rapid progress to a baby's feeding bottle with a teat at one end and a rubber valve on the other. He became the family pet, and one of my younger brothers insisted that the piglet was his. We taught him little tricks such as going through a dark tunnel, to investigate our pockets with his snout, to be rewarded by finding a tit-bit, and to sit on his haunches like a dog. We also made him climb a steep mound of mixed culm, to see him negotiating the downward slope on his backside with his front legs stiff as ramrods to retard his downward progress. I'd swear he was grinning happily as he made his comic descent. He had harness made for him, and wherever we went he came too, a pretty sight with patches of red dominating his hide. He put on weight so rapidly, that it was decided to fatten him as an extra, and have him slaughtered about March. All this was kept from us children and especially from my brother, his nominal owner. One day the Tamworth red was slaughtered and there was a terrific scene of grief and anger. My brother refused to touch any of the meat, and we were terribly sorry about it all, and wished with all our hearts that another solution had been possible. . .

The best known of all Welsh ballads concerns the sudden death of a black pig. It was composed by the Rev. John Owen c. 1854 when he was in service with Mr. and Mrs. James of Felin Wrdan, Eglwyswrw. The tragic disaster befell Dafi Thomas, Parcymaes, Brynberian. But the author of this inspired work recorded in his MS. Autobiography,[1] 'I wrote "Y Mochyn Du", now so well known throughout the land ; a song that will continue to corrupt the tastes of our young people when the tongue that first sang it will have long been silent in the grave. Forgive, O Lord, the sins of my youth ! '

The sad fate of the tame Tamworth Red, treacherously slain by those who nursed, fed and cosseted him, should also have been enshrined in a ballad entitled,—*Y Mochyn Coch*,—the Red Pig. It is too late now ; feelings have been blunted, and the bitterness of the circumstances have become nothing more than a faded memory.

---

[1]See *Dictionary of Welsh Biography* 714. Contribution by Dillwyn Miles.

LOVE IN A WELSH CLIMATE

THE Welsh of my day were all for Love, but indulgence in it was fraught with many perils, physical, social, moral and hypocritical. It was much easier for the Squire, especially if he was not a fluent Welsh speaker, to enjoy a fair spread of sin—than for the Welsh peasant. A communicating non-conformist say a Baptist or a Methodist—if caught out in illicit love, had to bear the sanction of ex-communication by the minister, deacons and the baptised members in congregation assembled. I remember one such transgressor being asked by the minister and the deacons, if he had anything to say before being cast out, ' Well ', he said, ' the only difference between some of you and me is, that I was caught ! ' The Squire if he was C. of E. had an easy time ; besides he was usually financially able to compensate the female sharer of his pleasures. I remember as a schoolboy being shown a terrace of brick houses—each with the key-stone of the arch above its front door in the shape of a most artistic Cupid, and being told that the rich owner of a brickworks had built them to house his brood mares as it were, and the legend was that all passes by him at pretty maids were welcomed. There was one proviso—they did not enter one of these houses until there was ample external evidence that the connection had been fruitful. I have a faint memory of seeing the old gentleman standing at the door of his house studying form on market day. Physically he now needed a stick, but there was still a sparkle in the eye, as he doffed his three-quarter, not a top hat to the ladies.

It is of course quite untrue to suggest that the little maids in service at the Plas or mansion, who were seduced were always the unwilling victim of the *Y Sgweier* or rich farmer ; often there was collusion as well as mutual delight. The words the soldiers sang, ' She was poor, but she was honest, Victim of the squire's whim, etc.', did not always apply. There were some men who were irresistable—often leading lights in church or chapel. Farmers hired maids and farm hands by the year—the hiring day being Michaelmas Fair on 10 November, when the future employer would seal the contract of service by an earnest *ern* of a shilling, sometimes 2/6—paid as a rule to the parents of the girl or youth to be hired. If later the employer for some reason did not choose to have the servant he would tell him so, and he'd keep the *ern.* Likewise the servant was released by returning the *ern.* It was the easiest thing in the world for a bachelor farmer with a young housekeeper and perhaps another couple of milk-maids, to find his way into their beds without much trouble. Then there were affairs between the head carters or plough men, ' y gwas mawr ', and maids on their own, or neighbouring farms. Girls were ' dated ' at chapel, concerts, eisteddfodau, singing festivals, and at harvest time. There were some who believed that no maid was more easily seduced than she who had been to an emotional prayer meeting, or a sermon with a *hwyl,* or above all a singing festival. A good intake of Handel or Bach would apparently lower the lady's defences sufficiently for her to stoop to folly. Tutors at theological colleges would advise their students not to go a-courting on Sunday, an emotional day, when *les girls* were most inclined to be permissive. During the winter months a singing rehearsal was held after the evening service, to get ready for the singing festival the following June. The likely lads would escort the chosen and willing back home to the farms often 2 or 4 miles away with the last part of the journey nearly always down an unmetalled rutted farm lane. There would be connivance by the employer at the late arrival home of his maid servant. Then there was the old established *Caru trwy'r nos* or ' Courting all night '. The girl would leave a ladder conveniently placed near or beneath her bedroom window and usually on a Saturday night the man of her choice would arrive, clean-shaven and smelling of scented soap, his Amlwch shag-tobacco-laden breath disguised by the heavy exotic perfume of ' Sen-Sen ' cachous. He would strip to his vest and long drawers both of heavy Welsh wool with a black vertical stripe in the drawers, and then with the nice protection of a blanket between them they'd commence to giggle and cuddle, protest and counterprotest, all very pleasurable no doubt. Occasionally the blanket proved insufficient insulation, and some months later a hurried marriage would be arranged—with the whole community rejoicing and congratulating the happy virile couple. Some of the happiest and most successful marriages in Wales have started on this basis. There was something similar in Scotland. I was once told of a Scottish minister who visited a fellow minister tending a flock out in the wilds, and whose house had only one bed, a big double one. Big enough for two, but did his comely housekeeper share it he was asked. ' Aye she does that, but dinna worry for we have a solid oak plank between us '. ' Are ye not tempted occasionally ? ' ' Aye that we are, but we bear it ! ' ' And when ye are surely tempted what do you do, do ye pray ? ' ' Och no, when we're sae sarely tempted, we just take the wee plank awa'.'

There were humorous episodes too. One old wag would wait till the boy friend had climbed the ladder, and was safely in the arms of his beloved, when he would quietly remove the means of escape and the poor lad would have to come down through the house, and meet the master on the way. Then there was the bachelor minister who fancied the young wife of one of his flock, and when her husband had gone to work, together they would keep the bed warm for a further period. One day the husband had to return for something he had forgotten, and found his wife and the man of God in bed together. She made the successful plea that she had been unable to resist the advances of the holy one ' y gŵr duwiol ' and her husband forgave her. But the holy one was soon afterwards again caught *in flagranta* and to avoid a scandal he agreed to accept a call to another chapel two counties away. He was a man of many parts, whose capacity to pray and preach always attracted a full house. He had something Chaucerian in his character, and withal he was a most worthy man in his profession. Women have always shown inability to resist the advances of men of God. There was the interesting case of Lawrence Clarkson the Dipper who in the 17th century preached that ' Unto the pure all things are pure ' (Titus I. 15) and that until you can lie with all women as one woman, and not judge it sin, you can do nothing but sin. There was a steady stream of women volunteers from his congregations ready to test the liberating effect of this doctrine. Unfortunately there were kill-joys in positions of authority who did not agree with his teachings, so Mr. Clarkson was arraigned for lying with the maids he had baptised.

Many illustrious Welshmen have had an irresistible appetite for women, a craving which was to them as necessary as food and vitamins. Often to a man with this need—to go to bed with a witty pretty woman was a biological necessity, and it was not interpreted as marital infidelity. Men have figured in Honours Lists because they had attractive and flexible wives, who proved irresistible to someone walking the corridors of power, not as a reward for their own intrinsic worth or work. The attitude of the Chapel towards those of its communicants who had loved not wisely but too well, was pompous, hypocritical and rather ridiculous. I recall a case being dealt with in the Gyfeillach of our Baptist Chapel when a girl had given birth to a fine baby some time previously came to plead for her place back, i.e. to be restored to the status of a full communicating member again. The minister reviewed the details of ' our sister who has transgressed and fallen, etc., etc., and who is now conscious of her great sin, etc., and who has now come in all humility, etc., etc., to beg to be accepted again as one of the community of God, etc. Did it accord with the wishes of the Gyfeilach for her to be re-admitted ? ' She was re-admitted nem con—and everybody congratulated her, while secretly a few envied her recent experience. Never once did I attend these degrading meetings without a feeling of spiritual nausea. I thought then it was a lot of hypocritical nonsense—and I still think so. Of course, there were the dauntless exceptions—those who defiantly bore the fruits of their love and said outright ' I shall never beg for my place back '. I saw such a grand old girl last year, when she was over 90 years of age—her memory of the last 30 years very dim, but she could tell me all about my childhood years, so I suspect she remembered well the days when Love was triumphant in her life. There was the true story in connection with this casting out of the company of communicants, in this case members of an Independant Chapel.The Elders with the minister were discussing their future action in respect of three of their girls and two youths, all members who had gone *dros clawdd* ' gone over the hedge '. The old blacksmith and farrier who was an acknowledged expert on ' breaking in ' ' torri mewn ' horses said his piece, ' Reverend I am no theologian as you know, but they do say I know something about horses. We break spirited young ones in not ' break them out ' ; which in Welsh is ' torri nhw i mewn, nid torri nhw maes ', the same verb meaning *break* and *expel.* Illicit conception took place quite often at harvest time, not in narrow bed, but savouring all heaven's delight beneath the open sky with the gentle dew a benediction from above. After all the omens were favourable—a hunters moon, a stomach full of home brewed beer, cooked meat, and vegetables—an excuse to go together to collect the odd handrake deliberately left behind in one of the fields—the laborious hours since 5 in the morning—and with the end of day, relaxation, and the natural upsurge of healthy animal spirits. And they could well ask what else was there for them to do.

Perhaps the most felicitous development of mutual love concerns a dear friend of mine—whose name and distinctions occupy half a column of Who's Who. His parents did not marry—but their love lasted the whole of their lives, and they were a model family in every way.

PASSIONATE ENCOUNTER

TROUT tickling was not only a skilled occupation, but in war-time with its attendant food scarcity, it was a profitable one. On a beautiful Summer's day, after tea, I was working the river downwards in its steep narrow valley. I was clad in corduroy knickerbockers which were rolled up above the knee, and a thin flannelette shirt. Vests and underpants were not then in fashion.

I was approaching the place where the back-fill of water from a dam which had been built to provide water power for a woollen-factory and a mill made the pools progressively too deep for wading, so I divested myself of my two garments which I rolled up and placed in a convenient crotch of a hazel tree. Then I waded and finally swam in the deep waters of the lake—the sides of which were enchanting green bowers formed by branches and leaves of beech, alder, and hazel which grew not like Keats's tall green rob'd senators of mighty woods, but were a tangled mass of greenery. The sides had been scooped by the scouring winter floods, so that the banks overhung the water—sustained by a riot of roots like a den of snakes, some fat and long squeezing Laocoon to death,—others their juvenile offspring. Suddenly I became aware of voices and the sound of footsteps above my head, and I was very much aware that I was naked. The obvious reaction was to hide and await for the intruders to pass. I edged quietly into the water under the bank, only my head out of the water, with my body resting on a mighty root. The voices sounded much nearer, but the sound of footsteps had ceased, so I knew the worst,—the unknown persons were walking on the sorrel-studded carpet of moss which covered a tiny headland directly opposite my hiding place. I peered out cautiously from behind a yashmak of soft silken green beechleaves. My escape was so effectively cut off that I unwittingly became a captive observer of what happened next. The alternative would have been to disclose myself, in all my nakedness, and this I was far too shy to do in the presence of the couple who had now sat down on their mossy couch. One was a young officer in mufti, and his companion a very pretty Irish girl who had come over to help on one of the farms deprived of male labourers by the war. They were a handsome pair, perfectly matched, and even to my inexperienced eyes, they were terribly in love with each other. They kissed and cuddled and murmured softly. Their passion waxed, and they seemed to mutually understand that the point of no return had been reached, even passed. Suddenly she pushed him away—and said, ' Oh, darling, I don't think we should have any clothes on ! ' These were the days before the invention of ' bras ' or foundation garments ; indeed, this beautiful creature had no need of any such artificial aids to enhance her generous endowment of natural beauty. They both stood up, and swiftly removed their clothing. They became locked in a melting embrace—sank slowly and gently on to their soft nuptial bed of moss. There was a gasp and a sigh of contentment when she was penetrated, and then stark passion almost frightening to see, took command. There were protestations of love, sweet moans, strokings, and mock bitings. The feeling these two untutored lovers had for one another, made them perform the act of love like accomplished practitioners, but with a tempo far fiercer than the classic encounter described by Thomas Carew :[1]

' Now in more subtile wreathes I will entwine
My sinowie thighes, my legs and armes with thine ;
Thou like a sea of milke shall lye display'd
While I the smooth, calme Ocean, invade
With such a tempest, as when *Jove* of old
Fell downe on *Danae* in a storme of gold ;
Yet my tall Pine, shall in the *Cyprian* straight
Ride safe at Anchor, and unlade her fraight :
My Rudder, with thy bold hand, like a tryde,
And skilfull Pilot, thou shall steere, and guide
My Bark into Loves channell, where it shall
Dance, as the bounding waves doe rise or fall :
Then shall thy circling armes, embrace and clip
My willing bodie, and thy balmie lip
Like a religious incence shall consume,
And send up holy vapours, to those powres
That blesse our loves, and crowne our sportfull houres,
That with such Halcion calmenesse, fix our soules
In steadfast peace, as no affright controules '.

---

[1] *A Rapture*, p. 49. *The Poems of Thomas Carew.* O.U.P., 1949.

The climax having been reached and passed, I had hopes they would go away, and let me escape, but no, for after a period of placid calm their passion was again aroused, again it flamed, and there they were again, for a longer period than before, imparadised in each other's arms. Satisfied at last, they leisurely dressed, and like another male and female many thousand years ago, ' they hand in hand with wandering steps and slow, Through Eden took their solitarie way '. Did they feel that time was running out on them ? Who knows, but in less than a month the sad news came that this boy had been killed in action in France. The girl left the district soon after, presumably for Ireland ; I never discovered whether this passionate encounter bore fruit. She was a lovely, generous creature who gave her all to him, and he to her, as well as his life for his homeland. Of such as these, too, is the kingdom of heaven, and it is a perpetually brave new world that breeds such people. Meanwhile the departure of these lovers released me from my immersion which had become uncomfortably chilly. I proceeded homeward pondering, but I never disclosed to a single soul what I had inadvertently witnessed. I felt it was something most personal to them, and a third person like myself had no right to share any of it. Many years passed, and I was in the monastery of St. Anthony in the Red Sea Desert, when I recalled, how a long time ago I was immersed, but not from choice, on one hot summer afternoon, whereas St. Anthony himself, from choice, made a habit of immersing himself in cool wells, to resist the salacious visions which assailed his holy spirit. To combat the visitations of sexual temptation he and others of the Desert Fathers went to ridiculous lengths to immolate their bodies, and as it was all in the mind it was very pointless !

' *Donne, preti, e polli non son mai satolli* ', Italian proverb, ' *Women, priests, and poultry are never satisfied* '.

Very few holdings could afford to keep expensive pedigree bulls, and fewer still, the capital tied up in a Clydesdale stallion, but there was one farmer, a widow, who kept two bulls, one Hereford the other a vicious Guernsey, whose bad temper no amount of sex could improve. She also owned a magnificent stallion which clomped on its rounds proudly beribboned in the charge of a Rabelaisian groom. This widow endured her lot in a merry way. She was always well-dressed, usually in a costume with a hand-embroidered silk blouse, and even in those early days, no woollen stockings but pure silk of a subdued hue. On her feet she usually wore neat dark-brown brogues, and on her head, when she went out, a natty green velour hat, in the band of which she had stuck a blue jay feather. A woman of dash and taste ; gay. She always came out to see the encounters between the bulls and the cows yearning for consummation, and she inevitably insisted on two mountings, although she must have known that one was just as likely to be fruitful. If the man who had brought the cow to bull, pleased her, she would take him up to the landing of the storehouse steps overlooking the stock-yard to watch the fun. When finally, after sniffing, curling up his nose, and observing any other preliminaries which etiquette decreed a properly-bred bull should observe, the gorgeous creature would mount and deliver his mighty thrust, she'd clasp her magnificent breasts, and exclaim if it was a heifer's first experience, 'O ferch fach i, dyna frathiad greulon !' 'O my poor girl that was a cruel stab !' But her more usual rejoiner was to lean on the man just enough to establish communication, and *sotto voce* utter something bucolic like, 'O what a magnificent stab—I'd be frightened to death if someone did that to me !' If the Barkis of that day was willing, he would be invited inside, to have a glass of something, and the opportunity to prove his mettle. This attractive widow was a kind and nice person. She had not destroyed her husband in bed ; the dreaded T.B. or consumption had done that before they had had a year of married joy. Nevertheless, the local connoisseurs believed that the late departed would have needed all his reserves of strength to survive love's battles with the lady he had chosen. She was not a Thaïs nor a Cleopatra, but a thoroughly pleasant female who adored the male, who would have been quite out of place on Lesbos. When her stallion had a date with someone's mare, she was there to enjoy the occasion, and as always impeccably attired. It was as if she were present at some ancient fertility rite of sacrifice, only this was no sacrifice. When the noble stallion, full of pride, puissance, heat and determination, decided the time had come for him to consummate the meeting, he would often be clumsy and lack accuracy. Guidance was then supplied by the groom, who having done this task would then lean his cheek against the mare's flank, remarking the while,—'Bois bach, I can hear it coming in like the Severn bore '. I never heard him vary this remark, so it must have been part of his permanent patter. The lady, while this was going on, would coyly comment on how soothing the unhurried fulfilment of sex between two horses was. Then naughtily she'd confess that she believed in guidance too, in fact, it was her strong point. The ball was now truly in the court of the mare's owner, and it was up to him to diffidently riposte with respect that perhaps his was the strong point, and, Yes, of course, hers the guidance. Country ways, maybe, but clearly understood and enjoyed by both parties.

Such sexy ladies have always been with us. John Aubrey[1] relates that another such was Mary Countess of Pembroke, sister of Sir Philip Sydney who 'was very salacious, and she had a contrivance, that in the Spring of the years when the Stallions were to leape the mares, they were to be brought before such a part of the house, where she had a vidette (a hole to peepe out at) to look on them, and please her selfe with their sport ; and then she would act the like sport her selfe with her stallions, one of her great Gallants was Crookeback't Cecill E of Salisbury '.

Sex has been around for quite a time, and if, as someone alleged, it has an ugly head, this has had no apparent effect on its undiminishing appeal throughout the ages. Sex is here to stay—its wondrous charm is constantly being re-discovered, in unexpected places,—by unexpected people. When the fiancée in Cincinatti of an American G.I. heard that he was carrying on with an English girl in London, whither he had been drafted, she wailed, 'What has she got which I haven't ?' He wrote back soothingly, 'Nothing honey, only she's got it right here !'

---

[1] *MS. Aubrey* 6, f. 81^{r}.

HAY HARVEST

Hay-making was one of the major events of the year, a gay time often a worrying time. A good hay harvest, and fodder for the animals in winter was assured, but a mouldy rick of hay was wasteful and not nourishing for beasts. In ancient times the gods would be propitiated so as to ensure a good harvest, but in Wales—the Almighty Himself was approached at His throne of grace to beg of Him sunny dry weather if it pleased Him, but if not then they would abide by His decision. The trouble was that the small-holder could not decide on the date to cut his crop ; there were other considerations, chief of which was the date the big farmers were going to cut theirs. In the days before the advent of the horse drawn hay cutting machine the work was done by scythe men, who were really the small holders come to help each other. The scythe is a wonderfully effective implement in the hands of an expert, and to see six or seven of them moving in a rhythmic éschelon was a glorious sight. As in Switzerland, they scythed on steep slopes as well as on the level ground. There was something hypnotic in the relentless non-stop rhythm. How welcome the halt to sharpen the long blade ! This was done by a rip or ripper, a flat piece of soft wood about 12 inches long, and about ¾ of an inch thick, with width varying from 3 to 4 inches and one end shaped into a comfortable handle. This board was spread with pig's grease, *bloneg*, on both sides, then sand—coarse on one side and fine on the other, rolled into the grease by a white stone ginger bottle, and the whole contrivance was carried at the scyther's back in a leather holster, the sand in the bottle, the grease in a tin all of which were attached to the holster by strings, or leather thongs. Later a ready made stone could be bought, which ultimately ousted the ripper. The scythes for mowing grass or hay had two doles or handles fixed to the snaith which had a double curve. The one with a cradle for cutting corn had only one handle—the lower one—and the snaith was much straighter but heavier. The wood used was ash, and we had several likely pieces drying out on the beams in the outhouse. The angle of the blade to the snaith was very much a matter of personal choice and was effected by wedging the blade at the required angle in the holding ring. Then a strutt of 1/4 inch iron which was attached to a hole in the foot of the blade with the other end shaped like a right angled hook, was driven by a stone or hammer into the snaith, and combined, these held the blade at the chosen angle.

Then came mechanisation with the Wood, Milwaukee, Deering, and other horse-drawn machines which made short work of a five or ten acre field. But they still could not cut the pightles, corners or slopes, so the scythe was not yet relegated to the museums. It took two good horses to draw these machines, but on my Grandfather's farm there was a big vicious raw-boned mule that could pull one of them by himself, an astounding example of traction power. The man who could afford a machine was the big farmer of the district, and in return for help with his own harvest, he would cut the hay of his neighbours. Again, the scyther was needed to cut the corners, and generally to tidy up. As soon as a field was cut, the hedges would be brushed and the thorns brambles and other weeds gathered, to make a *sail* or foundation for the rick. Beer had to be brewed against the probable date of the harvest, which if delayed by a spell of rain, meant a second brew. Every household brewed its own beer which was a wholesome nourishing drink. There was one farm where four brothers and their unmarried sister lived. They had beer for every meal, including breakfast, and their work output was phenomenal.

On 19 July 1906, mother paid 5/6 for a bushel of malt and 1/3 for a pound of hops. There was usually several gallons left over after harvest, and although the beer would progressively become flatter, it was a fine drink, and when we were children we were allowed a spoonful of demerara to sweeten it. It was not only the family that enjoyed this home-brewed beverage, for after a brewing, the pigs were given the malt and the hops mixed in their swill and a dusting of barley meal, and we would occasionally witness the edifying spectacle of a pig who too much had taken, and was so high, that dignified progress was impossible through frequently collapsing on to its hind quarters to the accompaniment of unmistakeable porcine laughter.

Most farmers grew oats, which was a hardy crop able to thrive on poor hill soil as well as survive bad weather. *Ceirch du bach,*—the short black oats—was the favourite. Apart from its value in feeding stock, oats when ground was an important food. It was made into griddle cakes, *sopas* which was buttermilk with oatmeal and usually some granulated sugar added, and that popular harvest dish *uwd* a kind of flummery. Uwd was the cooked juice of strained oatmeal. Mother loathed anything 'oaty' but father loved everything, including cakes, if made of oatmeal. He even went so far as to state, on no scientific evidence at all, that oats was better than any cereal for man, basing his contention on his knowledge of horses, and the importance of oats in their diet. Oats was once described by Dr. Johnson as a grain which in England is generally fed to horses, but in Scotland supports the people, on which Lord Ellibank commented, 'Very true and where will you find such *men* and such *horses* ?' The *uwd* was taken out to the haggard and the fields in huge tin milk dishes, in which it had set into a quivering brown blancmange. Everybody helped themselves to it, using wooden spoons and basins, adding to it either beer or cool fresh milk from the dairy. To supplement it, there were stacks of home made bread well-spread with salted butter. This was a most sensible midday repast, for the men and women were back at work within a quarter of an hour, a valuable saving of time when most harvests were not safely gathered in till dark. Although a mechanical horse-rake was invaluable in collecting most of the hay, yet there were always slopes, corners and hollows which only the busy hand-rakes of the women could effectively clear. These ladies worked all day clad in immaculate white aprons, well-laundered blouses, with their crowning glory, huge hats whose size was only exceeded by their feminine vanity, and fidelity to what was considered by them to be the fashion. As many as two dozen of them could be seen in a hayfield at one time, and the badinage went on all day between them and the men who were carting, pitching, or cocking. The banter and the laughter helped to bring the harvest home quite as much as the beer and ginger-pop. Often the Boss would take a hand-rake, and join the women and girls in the field, knowing that his presence would be a challenge and provide the opportunity for them to 'show-off'. Some old biddies would work twice as well then, while the saucy wenches would try to embarrass the master with remarks both risqué and witty. Sometimes it developed into a battle-royal twixt the pitchers, carters, and any other men in sight, and the witty ladies. Quick as a flash comment capped comment, double-entendres were so clad in apparent innocence that no covert bad taste could possibly be alleged. How they laughed ! But it kept them sane and happy. These good people worked from dawn till dark, yet their merry voices and gay laughter in the hay-fields could be heard all day long. To-day the tractor, with its multiple ancillary implements, has taken possession of these fields each in due season, and the noise of the tractor's exhaust has taken the place of human laughter and song. This seems to be a high price to pay for progress. In the rick yard there might be a mast with a pair of mechanical hooks, which could grab half a load of hay, and a strong horse would draw them up to the height required. A man with a pair of lines guided them and at the right moment released them. There was always an elder called the 'Gaffer' who was in charge of the construction of the rick. He instructed those on it to come out a little here, or take a piece back there, and so on, and it was he who would choose where to put the props, and when to slacken them as the hay subsided. He was the butt of the jokers who swore his upright was like a leaning house, but good rollicking humour prevailed till the last load was safely gathered in. Then the ladies handed round the beer to the men, and for the children there was home-made ginger beer fragrant with the yellow flowers of the herb agrimony.

A sense of achievement tinctured the satisfaction of the men gathering to come indoors to the great supper, which consisted of basins of cawl, huge plates of ham, beef and lamb, interlarding the new potatoes, young carrots, broad-beans and cabbage. The jugs of beer and milk on the tables were continuously replenished. After the orgy of meat there followed apple dumplings, or apple suet pudding, eaten with plenty of demerara sugar. These were eaten in large soup plates with the addition of cream or milk. The noisy leisurely repast over, there would be prognostication of the next day's weather when So and So were due to cart in their hay. By now John Barleycorn was stimulating the whole company to mirth, and there would be much 'sending' of one another home. I remember two brothers one weighing over 18 stone, proceeding home in the gloaming from haymaking. On reaching the footbridge across the river one solemnly warned the other that in the state they were in, it was dangerous to attempt to walk the plank. The other having accorded this caution solemn consideration agreed and they both plunged into the water which was up to their waists, and with the steadying aid of pitchforks, they waded across. On reaching the other side they congratulated themselves on their sagacity, for they could easily have slipped off the bridge and got wet! Another habit of farmers in those days emphasised the importance of a good hay harvest—if it came to rain after it was safely gathered in, they would stand in groups in the rain getting soaked to the skin, as if they were offering some primitive thanksgiving. I remember vividly such a scene—with our neighbour Evan mercilessly teasing our neighbour James for the fuss he had made when butted by the billy-goat which Evan kept on the farm to prevent contagious abortion. There we were about to go our several ways, when this dreadful animal appeared on the horizon—behind Evan, and he was preparing to charge. After all the leg-pulling nobody felt like shouting a warning so Evan received the full impact behind his knees, and down he went. We tried to pull his leg about it, but no—for the creature had mutined against his master and for this there was only one punishment. Evan walked solemnly to the house, emerged with a 12 bore gun, and shot the mutineer dead. His carcase hanged, drawn and quartered, proved to be the toughest venison of that year. Often the greatest leg-pullers are those who cannot bear to have their own legs pulled.

When the ricks or the stacks of hay had settled, and their final shape established by plucking their outsides, and placing what was thus garnered on top, to make a slope of not less than 45°, they were thatched with wheat straw, or if you had bog-land, with reeds. The straw was wetted then drawn to obliterate tangles, and a handful was twisted at one end and the thatching began from the eaves upwards. The straw ropes to hold down the thatch were twisted by a home-made gadget—a stock but instead of a bit just a hook to hold the straw. Pricks were cut from hazel wands and these were stuck through the straw rope deep into the hay, for in winter the wind often reached gale force. In addition heavy slabs of stone from the quarry were attached at regular intervals to the straw ropes. Although cocoanut fibre cords were available at reasonable prices, the old way persisted on most of the farms till well after the end of the War. After all it was an ancient art—Andrew Marvell describes how Ametas and Thestylis spent flirtatious moments making hay-ropes.—‘ Think'st Thou that this Rope would twine if we both should turn one way ? Where both parties so combine, Neither Love will twist nor Hay ’. The final touches to the thatch was to trim it with a pair of sheep-shears ; after all, the neighbours would be coming along to inspect, to criticise, to tease, and create some innocent merriment.

SOCIAL BACKGROUND

The social background of life from about the time of mother's birth can be traced in the old copies of the local newspaper,—*The Cardigan & Tivy-Side Advertiser*. Until the end of the First World War medicine was on the whole empirical ; a good doctor obeyed a few proven rules and applied his common sense. If he made a fatal mistake in dealing with a patient, the mistake was buried. It was the golden age of quack medicines, for there was no limit to the credulity of the masses. Their faith in their particular brand of pill, ointment or draught was touching, and no doubt this faith did more good than the specific they swallowed. John Williams, Chemist and Druggist, established in 1855 offered a liberal choice. In the 31 Jan. 1873 issue of the *Tivy Side* he advertised, 'John Williams begs to inform the gentry and inhabitants of the Town of Cardigan and its vicinity' that he could supply drugs and Patent Medicines carriage free. Presumably the gentry would lay down a cabinet or two of these 'goodies' against the evil days that might come. These are some items from Mr. Williams's list : Lambert's Asthmatic Balsam ; Ford's Balsam of Hore-hound ; Powell's Balsam of Aniseed ; Keating's Lozenges ; Locock's Lozenges, Holloway's Pills and Ointments ; Worsdell's Pills ; Cockle's Pills ; George's Pills ; King's Dandelion and Tonic Pills ; De Jongh's Cod Liver Oil ; Townsend's Sarsaparilla ; Dinnesford's Magnesia ; Lamplough's Pyretic Saline ; Floroline ; Godfrey's Extract of Elder Flowers ; Rowland's Kalydor ; Gowland's Lotion ; Mrs. Allen's Preparations ; 'Hair Dyes', etc. ; and all other Patent Medicines in Vogue. Mr. Williams was also the local agent for Thorley's Food for Cattle !

In 1873 justice was meted out impartially. Anne Lewis aged 29, a married woman who pleaded guilty to stealing a shoulder of mutton was sentenced to 5 months hard labour and 2 years supervision by the police. For an indecent assault on Ellen Hennessey, two men were acquitted, but for maiming a horse a man received 10 years penal servitude. Fines for drunkenness were 6d and costs. Affiliation orders averaged 3/- a week which could easily have been half the weekly wage of a labourer ; the price of sin was higher then than now. A J.P. was fined £5 for catching a salmon without a licence. For being drunk and disorderly at Cilgerran St. Lawrence's Fair a man was fined 7/6 and costs. Benjamin Griffiths was given a much heavier sentence for his conduct at the same Fair. It appeared that he had taken off his coat, vest, and hat and was offering to fight anybody. When Constable Morris advised him to go home, the witty Benjamin told him to go somewhere else, so the Law closed with him, receiving in the process blows in the face and kicks on his knee. The magistrates, unable to appreciate Benjamin's devastating sense of humour, sentenced him to 6 weeks hard labour. In 1873 the medical officer of the St. Dogmaels Union (workhouse) received £20 to £25 per annum ; the Master £100 ; a teacher £20 ; the Clerk £15.0.0 ; the Seamstress £5.0.0. The woman who cleaned the school-room in the workhouse received £3.18.0. Only reading was taught in it !

Workhouses in general were 19th century creations, but such institutions existed in the 17th century, special Acts being passed to authorise their construction. To understand how the Unions came about the fascinating story of the Poor Law from medieval times must briefly be told. The Church, religious houses, guilds, and manors were all involved, and the Parish was always the administrative unit. When the poor became poorer, they would also become ' rogues and vagabonds ' and would commit crimes against society, whereupon Acts were passed decreeing penalties such as whipping, ear-cropping and hanging. After the dissolution of the monasteries, the parish had to shoulder more of the burden of dealing with its poor, and the result was the great Elizabethan Act of 1601, which was to govern the poor-law administration for over two hundred years. In 1817 a Committee of the House of Parliament reported that the poor rate was increasing so fast that it would shortly absorb all the rents from land. This caused a national stir amounting almost to a panic, followed by the setting up of a Royal Commission, which speedily issued its Report condemning the whole system. So the Act of 1834 put an end to the parochial system of poor law administration, which had lasted so long, and amalgamated the parishes into *Unions*, which were governed by *Guardians*. Early in the 18th century Parliament had authorised the erection of ' Workhouses ' and our parish Llantood belonged to the Cardigan Board of Guardians with the workhouse at St. Dogmaels on the Pembrokeshire side of the river Teify. The Guardians with the Master and the Medical Officers met every other Thursday at 11 a.m. In 1898 about 30 tramps were admitted per fortnight while the number of inmates (paupers) was 49. The Poor Rate in 1894/5 varied from 1/6 to 2/- in the pound, and it was collected in March and in August. In our Union the rate was collected by William Rees, a man I remember when I was a boy, as a fascinating figure because he wore a Sherlock Holmes's fore and aft cap. To have to go through ill-health or indigence into the Workhouse was something to be avoided at all costs. It was a pathetic sight to see someone who had been unable to avoid this fate, stripped of pride, riddled with shame and steadily losing the desire to live. Life in the workhouse for a local unfortunate, was a killing experience and paupers did not on the whole live long. When they died they were buried in cheap coffins, and my mother recalled an occasion when a coffin came adrift, exposing the corpse within, and it had to be tied with rope before reaching its destination. Paupers or tramps were sometimes surprised by death while on the road, or lying in the straw at a farm. There was the disgraceful episode when a pauper was found dead by the roadside near Blaenffos when much difficulty was experienced in finding a clergyman willing to bury him in his churchyard. They all wished to know to what denomination if any, he belonged. Until this was known, there were no funeral rites for the stranger.

In 1894 the salary of a Headmaster was fixed by the School Board at £111.17.4. In 1897, he received £112.10.0, a rise of 12/8 in three years. The Headmistress averaged £84.8.8 per annum. Harvest ale was 1/- a gallon. A watch cost £5 to £15 ; a sewing machine £2.17.6. Dr. Tibbles offered his Vi-cocoa at 6d., 9d., and 1/6, with the exhortation, ' Give up drinking tea which, even if properly infused, is only a stimulant, and *not* a nourishing beverage '. A ridiculous mystique had grown up around tea—only the mistress was deemed competent to infuse it. A maid brought a locked tea-caddy to her mistress, and then the ceremony of infusing began. Mothers were offered Mrs. Winslow's Soothing Syrup for teething babies which guaranteed natural (?) quiet sleep ' by relieving the child from pain, and the little cherub awakes as bright as a button ', all for 1/1½ a bottle. Mrs. Winslow had to compete with the redoubtable German Nurse who invented Mother Siegel's Syrup, which it was claimed cured nine-tenths of all human ailments. At this time (1897) a leading local grocer, Bowen Bros., with branches at Cardigan, Pontypridd, and Newport, Pembs., was advertising ' Dessert and Goodies '. The word ' goody ' is an appropriate example of the rise and decline in the usage of a word. It was in common use seventy years ago, and then it faded until recent times when the younger generation resurrected it. In December 1897, John Foster, a pauper at the workhouse who hailed from Gateshead, was sentenced to one month's hard labour for destroying his bedclothes. Poor fellow ! he probably felt that any change, even prison could not be worse. At this time there were 49 inmates, with a steady turnover of 27-30 tramps per fortnight. Capt. William Jones's tender to supply culm for the workhouse was accepted at 6/3 a ton delivered. There was also a large number of paupers receiving out-door relief. In the chemists' shops you could now buy Dr. J. Collis Browne's Chlorodyne, D.C.L. Malt Extract, and Calves' Foot Jelly. I still associate the presence in the house of Calves' Foot Jelly with a critical illness in the family. When Father was so very ill with rheumatic fever both the Malt Extract, and the Calves' Foot Jelly were prescribed, thus amply confirming the serious nature of his illness.

To take a step forward towards the outbreak of the Great War, an event took place in May 1914 which affected the whole district ; it was the death of a most brilliant physician and surgeon, Dr. Evan Bowen at the age of 29. He was our family doctor, and we mourned his premature passing, as did the whole town and district. He qualified at Edinburgh in 1910, and during his stay at the University won most of the major prizes including the Gold Medal, the first Welshman to do so. 1914 was the year of the cheap Ford Motor Car, a 2 seater costing as little as £125; a 4 Seater Overland cost £275. In August 1914 you could get single false teeth for 5/- each and Upper or Lower ' cases ' for £2. After the declaration of War in August, the Company of the 4th Welsh Territorials returned hurriedly from summer camp. The first local casualty was a man from St. Dogmaels who was lost when the *Amphion* struck a mine. The Pembrokeshire Yeomanry mobilised at Tenby, and the Bishop of St. Asaph volunteered on the 14 August for active service at home or abroad. The public throughout the land were being told that the Germans were in headlong flight. In September more local casualties at the Front, but you could not slow up the queue of volunteers. Our clog-maker William Evans had his three sons with the colours, one of whom had been a guardsman in the Boer War. William Roch, brother of Walter the M.P., left for active service. He was to die later at Gallipoli with many of our local lads. The headlines blazened with pride the destructive work of British airman. By the end of October there were casualties among the county families of the district,—Major Colby of Ffynnone killed,

Lieut. Kemes Lloyd wounded, Capt. Gower, Castell-maelgwyn, taken prisoner. Kemes Lloyd was the son and heir of Sir Martein and Lady Lloyd of Bronwydd, and he was later killed in action in September 1916. In December one of the most colourful of local characters Twm Waunbwll died. What a character old Twm was! He used to come into Cardigan on market day by train, with a sack into which he put all the provisions for the week; meat, fish, tea, sugar being dumped together unceremoniously to be carried on his shoulder down to the station. One Saturday he arrived without his trousers. Apparently he had sat on an ant-hill, and in the train he began to itch. To get rid of the ants he took his trousers off, but while he was shaking them vigorously outside the window they filled with air and were wrenched from his grasp. Undeterred he carried out his shopping clad in his huge Welsh woollen long underpants with black longitudinal stripes. To test the effiicacy of grease he only treated one clog of the pair he was wearing to see which would last the longer. He found that the ungreased one did, so he never blackened his boots or clogs again. He was an old bachelor, though his mother once tried to teach him the first steps of courtship. ' Now Twm ', she said, ' I'll go upstairs ; you go outside, and throw up some gravel at the bedroom window '. So out he went, and threw up the gravel. His mother opened the window saying coyly, ' Who is there ? ' ' O dammo Mam ! ' he retorted, ' you know its me, for you only sent me out about a minute ago ! '

When his mother died he insisted she be buried just inside the gate of the churchyard, for as he told the minister, ' There'll be one hell of a rush to get out once the resurrection trumpet blows '. This eccentric old boy was full of kindness. He used to lend money to local farmers to buy their farms. If they made good he would waive the repayment of the capital.

The passing of Twm Waunbwll made us realise how refreshing it is to have one or two such characters in our midst. Unfortunately, we do not seem to breed such any more. Perhaps the atmosphere of this benevolent, sanction-ridden protective welfare society, is inimical to such and the instincts to become a ' character ' are stifled at birth.

Strangely enough the price of a Ford Runabout came down to £115, and to help the hypochondriacs, and the gullible to sustain the strain of a war, all these internal and external aids were on offer,—Hughes's Blood Pills, Doan's Backache Kidney Pills, Virol, Beecham's Pills, Hayman's Balsam, Gwilym Evans's Quinine Bitters, Gomer's Balm, which could cure anything on the skin, in the flesh, or in the bone, and Mother Siegel's syrup at 2/9 a bottle. Then there was Clarke's Blood Mixture which cured Scrofula, Bad Legs, Abscesses, Glandular Swellings, Boils, Pimples, Sores, Blood Poison, Piles, Rheumatism, Gout, etc., etc., at 2/9 a bottle with the exhortation to steadfastly refuse substitutes, but to take Clarke's B 41 Pills which were warranted to cure in either sex all acquired [V.D. ?] or constitutional Discharges from the Urinary Organs, Gravel, and Pains in the back ; in boxes at 4/6 each. Clarke's rival was Mr. J. E. George, M.R.P.S. of Hirwaun, Aberdare, whose Pile and Gravel Pills had stood the test of forty years, and sold at 1/1½ and 2/9 a box. Of these pills the Rev. J. C. Williams wrote that he had been using them with great benefit to himself for 2 or 3 years,—'May God spare your life ! I consider you to be a great benefactor of mankind'. Our local chemist, Mr. Howell Morgan, M.P.S., was not to be outdone ; he offered *Rista* powders at 1½d each, 'the greatest Remedy of the age' which cured Toothache, Headache, Rheumatism, Neuritis, etc., etc. 'Safe, sure, Palatable' he announced triumphantly. He really was a good chemist, and he had a large clientele who preferred his diagnosis and subsequent treatment to that of a medical man. 'I will make up a bottle for you', he'd say after listening to the sufferer's complaint. He would have done well in France or Switzerland where the Chemist does treat and prescribe.

The war soon affected agriculture. In November 1915 farm servants received the unprecedented wages of £35—£40 a year and their keep. Young boys could get £18-£25. There was a great scarcity of girls and women to undertake farm work, for the factories making munitions at Pembrey and Burry Port paid so much better. The price of cattle had also risen,—yearlings £7-£9, 2 year olds £9-£13, heifers £14-£16. Old fat cows £10-£14. In view of the farm labour shortage cream separators became popular. The *Diabolo* 15 gallons per hour cost £3.15.0, and the 82 gallons per hour £15.15.0 both with a free month's trial. The other well-known make was *Melotte* which was claimed to be the world's best separator as it extracted 20% to 40% more cream. We bought an Alfa-Laval separator which gave good service for many years. The only snag was the time spent on cleaning it twice a day.

The Cardigan 1st 4th Welsh were now at Suvla Bay awaiting the carnage, and the number of pupils on the books of the Grammar School rose to 235, which was a record. Two years later the roll reached 270, a new record.

SUNDAY SCHOOL AND CHAPEL

EVERY Sunday at 2 o'clock, all of us who were below a certain age, perhaps ten, attended school in the vestry of the Baptist chapel at Penybryn. This room was above the Chapel's stable, and was reached by an outside stone staircase. The main purpose of the Sunday School was to teach us how to read the Bible in Welsh. William Salesbury's *Testament Newydd* had appeared in 1567, and Dr. William Morgan's Welsh Bible in 1588, but only a few of the ordinary Welsh peasants had one. Queen Elizabeth had decreed in 1563 that the Bible should be translated into Welsh, under the supervision of the four Welsh Bishops, and the Bishop of Hereford, and copies placed in the parish churches under penalty of £40, to be levied on each of the Bishops. Episcopal apathy triumphed, and nothing happened until Dr. Morgan's edition of between 500 and 1000 copies in 1588. There was a 2nd edition by Bishop Parry in 1620, and this is our authorised version. In 1630 appeared vicar Pritchard's *Beibl bâch*, ' the little Bible ', at a price of 5/-, quite a sum for those days. Seventeen years later Vavasor Powel and Walter Cradoc issued 1000 vest pocket copies of the New Testament. Then in 1770 came Peter Williams's Bible, of which over thirty-eight editions have been printed. In 1800 we had the saga of Mary Jones, a Welsh girl who lived near Dolgelly, who was filled with the desire and determination to possess her own copy of the Bible. The nearest to her was in a farm house two miles away, but she heard that there were some Bibles for sale 25 miles away in Bala. So she saved and skimped till she had the price of the Holy Book, and then in her bare feet walked to Bala to Thomas Charles, who told her that all the copies were already sold or ordered. Grief overwhelmed her, but her distress so affected Thomas Charles that he spared her a copy. This was one of the 10,000 copies of the 1799 edition by the Clarendon Press. Thomas Charles now decided to ask the Council of the Religious Tract Society to supply Bibles for all Wales, whereupon Joseph Hughes replied that he would, and not only for Wales but for the whole world. Thus was born the British and Foreign Bible Society.

In the 18th-century, the success of the circulating schools of Griffith Jones was due to the intense desire of illiterate adults to learn how to read their Bibles. Mother used to tell me than when young couples married at seventeen or eighteen, they were always given a Bible, which was allocated a prominent place on the oak dresser, *y seld*, dusted daily, and on its fly-sheets would be recorded the marriages, births, and deaths of members of the family. It might be asked why the native tongue was not taught in the Board Schools, and the answer must be sought partly in the Report of the Commissioners in 1847 on the state of education in Wales. Much, if not most of the evidence was collected by parsons and by students of Lampeter College where students were trained for the Church, in those days, of England. The Rev. Griffith Thomas, Cardigan, felt that '. . . If Welsh children learn English they can themselves learn to read Welsh'. The Rev. Henry Lewis Davies, Troedyraur said that wages were 6d to 8d a day, and that among the females only one in six was chaste,—it would have been fascinating to hear him explain how he arrived at his figures ! All the Church of England clergy were against the chapels. It was stated (Part II IX 66) that ' the Welsh language is a vast drawback to Wales, and a manifold barrier to moral progress and commercial prosperity of the people. It is not easy to over-estimate its evil effects '. A teacher was usually paid £12 to £13 per annum. The fees charged were 3/- a quarter for Reading and Writing, an extra shilling if Arithmetic was included and for another shilling geography and English grammar were taught as well. The Rev. David Charles put the nonconformist point of view (871, p. 21), ' The people require schools unattached to any one creed. They regard liberty for their children to attend their own places of worship on the Sabbath as of the highest importance ; it would therefore be desireable that, whatever Government aid be given, it be applied in such a manner as to secure this. I believe that were means to erect school-houses supplied, it would in general be sufficient, and education be greatly promoted '. The conclusions of the Commissioners were that the Welsh language and the religious nonconformity were the causes of ignorance and immorality in Wales. These mistaken conclusions rankled and festered in the minds of the Welsh people—and the Report, became known as the ' Treachery of the Blue Books '. Therefore staunch Baptist parents saw to it that their children attended Sunday School from an early age to learn Welsh, which was so inadequately taught in the State schools. I look back with gratitude and affection to the years I spent every Sunday afternoon being taught by two gentle ladies. The first lesson was to learn the Welsh alphabet which is phonetic. The letters were in prominent black with an explanatory sketch underneath each. For instance, **ll** had the picture of a spoon, which in Welsh is *llwy* ; **p** had a peacock, a *paun*. When we had mastered the alphabet, we proceeded to the next sheet which had lists of simple words offering little difficulty, *dwr*—water ; *bara*—bread ; *gwin*—wine ; *glân*—pure ; *tân*—fire ; *mam*—mother ; *tad*—father ; *chwaer*—sister ; *brawd*—brother ; *ych*—ox, which we called *bustach*, but in the Bible is *ych*. As time went on the vocabularies included more Biblical words, and more difficult words. When we passed out of one class to a higher one—we were given little books as presents. The great day eventually came when we were promoted to be the most junior group in the Chapel itself, where there might be five or six study groups. We studied a selected chapter from the Bible, and each one of us read a verse in turn, after which you had to explain it to your teacher. The system seems to have worked well enough, for most of the instructors were competent, and had done their home-work in advance. The school closed with a prayer, followed by a hymn—the most popular being '*Am yr ysgol rad Sabothol, clod, clod, i Dduw*', 'For the free Sunday School, praise, praise to God'. 'In it we get the best instruction,—the perfect instruction of the Book of books, For having this in our mother's tongue, praise, praise to God'. These words by the Rev. Roger Edwards were sung to the lilting melody of 'Wynnstay', composed by J. A. Lloyd in 1871. This tune has also become a favourite with the Salvation Army who have a ear for a catchy tune.

The Baptist cause in North Pembrokeshire at this time was flourishing. The oldest church was at Rhydwilym just inside the county of Carmarthen ; incorporated in 1668 when persecution of Nonconformists was raging. In seaside places like Swansea the danger at the beginning of the 18th century was from the Press gangs who descended on the meetings, and took away the young male Baptists for service in the Navy. This caused many to emigrate to America, especially to Philadelphia. Our chapel at Penybryn was not opened till 1819, but not more than two or three miles distant were big Baptist chapels, the oldest of which was at Cilfowyr, which was incorporated in 1704. Previously the faithful of Cilfowyr had met at the house of Lettis Mortimer who married Edward Morgan. It was their son who donated the land for the chapel and churchyard. Meetings were held in a dwelling house called Rhosgerdd in St. Dogmaels, which sponsored by Cilfowyr became

Blaenywaun Chapel, opened in 1745, with 27 members. This first edifice had a thatched roof. Ebenezer, Dyfed, was opened in 1768, and Bethania, Cardigan in 1775. By 1777 the membership at Ebenezer had reached 135, and by 1795 the total was 340, a clear indication of the rapid growth of the Baptist cause in this rural area. Meanwhile in *Tŷ'r Iet* the house of John Michael, a deacon at Ebenezer, services were held, and also in houses near Bridell called Penfeidr and Penralltcadwgan. The people who lived at Penralltcadwgan were Dissenters, and it was not long before differences arose, and the Baptist members turned their faces towards Bridell and Penybryn, longing for a place of worship of their own, not shared by any other denomination. Their wishes were met in 1818, when Thomas Williams, farmer and carrier, of *Glanpwllafon* granted them a lease of land at Penybryn for 5,000 years on payment of one shilling a year, for the purpose of erecting a place to worship in accordance with the manner and beliefs of particular baptists, who were also to have access to the baptistry to be constructed in the river at *Glanpwllafon* running through the field of Parknewydd-bach, and the use of the said stream of water. On the fourteenth of May 1818 work on the new chapel commenced. Exactly a year later on the 13 May 1819 it was officially opened, the lesson being read by Rev. James James, Hermon, Prayer by Rev. David Mathias, Cardigan, and sermons by the Revs. David Phillipps, Blaenywaun ; Ben Davies, Cilfowyr and John Herring, of Cardigan. The first to be baptised on 27 June 1819 was Elizabeth Williams, the wife of Thomas Williams who had given the land. She was then 80 years of age. For the first fifteen years Penybryn was under the wing of Ebenezer, whose Minister was the Rev. W. R. Davies. In 1833, when its membership had reached 65 Penybryn became a full member of the Baptist Association. One of the deacons appointed in 1838 was David Toby who kept a ' smuggling ' tavern in Ivy Cottage, where in my day, my great friend Andrew Williams lived. The first minister was the Rev. Jesse Jones, but he was given a year's notice and he left in 1843. It appears that there was considerable dissention and strife in the congregation, and unfortunately the senior deacon Thomas Griffiths, Glynhenllan—uchaf died, who was the only person with sufficient sense and authority to deal with such events. The following year Ben Williams and David Edwards were cast out of membership for unseemly behaviour at the St. Lawrence's Fair in Cilgerran. In 1850 the Rev. Morris Evans came to take joint charge of Penybryn and Penuel, Cilgerran. His stipend was £25 a year, a crown per week from each chapel, and he had to find his own food and raiment! On the 9 December 1853 William Williams their oldest member died aged 102. John George of *Ffynnoncoranau* took the subject of his funeral oration, 'With long life will I satisfy him, and shew him my salvation'. The Welsh version in this instance is more poetic,—'*Digonaf ef a hir ddyddiau a dangosaf iddo fy iachawdwriaeth*'. The old chapel building at Penybryn was pulled down in 1869. In 1871 the new minister for Penybryn and Cilgerran received 8/6 a week from each church, making £44.4.0 a year. The new chapel was opened on Christmas Day 1871, its total cost of £400.7.6 having been collected before that date plus a testimonial of five guineas to the minister. This was at a time when servants' wages in the district were never more than 4d a day! The pulpit used was the pulpit of old Bethania, Cardigan. The vestry was built with the stones from the demolished first chapel, and one of the seats too came from the same place. A thriving Young People's Society was formed under the chairmanship of Jonathan George, a man of tremendous natural endowment, poet, bard, preacher, and an orator with a natural flair for politics. Two young persons John John, and John Rees, who were farm labourers at Broyan, and William Evans farm servant at *Penralltddu*, began to preach, and became Baptist ministers. An application to be allowed to have a day school in the chapel was refused, but after the erection of the vestry, permission to hold it there was granted, and it was conducted by Margaret Griffiths. William Lewis, who made my grandmother's coffin, was made a deacon in February 1884. At this time the Chapel choir was famous for its singing, led by Thomas Morris, Broyan, and it held concerts throughout the district. The quartette was famous locally, its members being Thomas Morris, Jonathan George and the two daughters of John Lewis of *Gaer* by Broyan Mill. In 1885 the Rev. William Evans, a good musician came to take charge of the two churches, and his salary was £6 for every 4 weeks. One of the ministers at the meeting to settle him in *cwrdd sefydlu*, the induction service was the famous R. D. Roberts, Llwynhendy.

One of the 'characters' at this time was Dafydd Owen, a 'whipper-in' by profession for Glanrhyd Board School which my father attended. He was famous for his eloquent impromptu prayers, and was much in demand to open big meetings. Those who remember him say that he closely resembled Lloyd George in physical appearance. He was precentor and sang with one foot on the big seat, and most of the time with his eyes tightly shut. Doubtless his soul was refreshed by visions of the promised land, the Avallon of the Pilgrims, which Islwyn described so superbly in his famous hymn,—'*Gwêl uwchlaw cymylau amser, O fy enaid! gwêl y tir Lle mae'r awel fyth yn dyner, Lle mae'r wybren fyth yn glir; Hapus dyrfa, Sydd yn nofio yn ei hedd*'. 'Look beyond the clouds of Time, O my soul! to see the land where the breeze is always gentle, where the sky is always clear. Happy multitude, who are basking in its peace'. When Miriam Jones died in 1894 she left £30 to the 'Cause' at Penybryn. In this year too, a new minister, the Rev. Edwin Watkin, took charge of the two churches. At his induction service, the big 'guns' were in action,—the Revs. John Williams, Bethania; W. A. Williams, Ferry Side; Aaron Morgan, Blaenffos; E. T. Jones, Llwynpia and R. B. Jones, Caersalem, Llanelli. These services were long remembered in the district, and my mother often talked about them with proper Baptist pride. At this time too, the Bible class and the temperance meetings were flourishing. Three of the young members became Baptist ministers; visible fruit of the Sunday School and the Prayer Meetings of the Baptist cause at Penybryn. The Rev. Edwin Watkins left in 1901; I can remember him from the photograph which Mother had,—and he was succeeded by his namesake Rev. J. Glyndwr Watkins, who was the minister during the Revival of 1904-5. There is an endemic quality about religious revivals, and from 1858 there had been sporadic outbreaks. In 1873 the two evangelists Moody and Sankey came to England to preach and to sing the Gospel. In spite of the considerable prejudice against Sankey's harmonium, and towards his Negro Jubilee Singers, they were soon claiming to have made 1400 converts, mostly women. A clown at a musical hall would say, 'I feel rather moody', to which his partner would reply, 'And I rather Sankey-monious'. It was the spirited singing that fetched in the converts. Some of the tunes were very catchy, especially—'Hold the Fort for I am coming', 'Safe in the arms of Jesus', 'The Great Physician', 'In the sweet by and by', 'I am coming Lord, Coming now to Thee', 'Wash me, cleanse me, in the blood that flowed on Calvary', 'Tell me the Old, Old Story', 'Stand up, stand up for Jesus, Ye soldiers of the Cross', 'I love to tell the Story', 'There were ninety and nine that safely lay, In the shelter of the fold', 'Work for the night is coming', 'Jesus loves me, This I know, For the Bible tells me so', 'I need Thee every hour', 'Oh where is my wandering boy tonight'. When we were young, uncritical, and full of energy we sang these songs or hymns with uninhibited gusto. I still like them, just as I like a good sing-song by the admirable Salvation (Sally) Army accompanied by their big brass, with their guernsies proudly worn.

The 1904/5 Revival[1] in Wales was a more emphatic affair, concentrated on certain personalities, the most important of whom was Evan Roberts. However he was not the originator of the movement in West Wales, which was started at a Methodist chapel in New Quay, about eighteen miles north of Cardigan town.

It was at a Christian Endeavour meeting, when Florrie Evans, a young girl, stood up and said, ' I love Jesus with all my heart ! ' A revival had been prayed for and expected, and others became infected by the vision and the ecstasy. Accompanied by the Rev. Seth Joshua, a brake-load of the New Quay revivalists went to Newcastle Emlyn to form a mission, but they found Newcastle a hard nut to crack. Prayer was intensified, and the Almighty was invited to ' Bend us O Lord ', *Plyg ni O Arglwydd.* These meetings at which Florrie Evans and Maude Davies sang and testified were attended by a young man, Evan Roberts, who was much impressed. He was a student at a Prep. School and lived in lodgings. Here in his bedroom he had a Vision, and Light filled his room. He prayed so fervently and so long that his landlady turned him out for she felt sure he was mad or possessed. Even before he went to Newcastle Emlyn he would wake up at 1 o'clock and for hours as many as four or five, have intimate talks with God. For a month after arriving in Newcastle Emlyn, God chose not to appear. Then God—not Jesus Christ, showed himself to Evan, and told him to return to Loughor to speak to his own people. Evan delayed, but in the Chapel he heard God commanding him to go. He replied, ' Lord if it is Thy will I shall go '. Instantly the whole place was filled with a dazzling light. So he went back to his village, and invited the youths to meet him. They were at first reluctant to listen to him but at last six of them declared for Jesus. This did not satisfy him, so he kept on praying, ' Oh Lord, give me six more—I must have six more ! ' They all prayed together and he got his second batch of six. The news spread like wildfire, and soon he was conducting at least three meetings a day. These would last from 7 p.m. till 4.30 a.m. The fall-off in takings at the public houses was

[1]See *The Revival in the West*, a 64 pp. penny pamphlet by W. T. Stead, 1905. *Life Story of Evan Roberts and Stirring Experiences in the Welsh Revival*, 96 pp., 6d. by Rev. W. Percy Hicks, 1906.

remarkable, attendance dropping from 300 to 6, and the takings adding up to barely £5 instead of the usual £40. Thieves, drunkards, prizefighters were now working on God's side. Brewers complained they had lost 75% of their trade. Contrary to popular belief, Evan Roberts did not preach much ; most of the hypnotism and subsequent conversion emanated from mass singing and prayer. He had his attendant singing ladies, Maggie Davies, Annie Davies, S. A. Davies, Annie Rees, and a professional, May John, R.A.M., whose rendering of '*Dyma gariad fel y moroedd, Tosturiaethau fel y lli*', 'Here is Love like mighty oceans, Here are mercies like the flood', was very effective. Cardiff at this time was credited with 4,000 prostitutes. Two of them, drunk, were taken by a workman to a meeting at Tabernacle Chapel. When the congregation sang, 'Jesu Lover of my soul', one of them took a bottle of whisky from her pocket and it was at once carried outside and ostentatiously poured into the gutter. The newly converted would appeal to others to join them, very much in the manner of the tailess fox of Aesop's fable. The hymn of the '59 Revival was resurrected, '*Y Gŵr a fu gynt o dan hoelion*', 'The Man who was once nailed'. Evan insisted that it was not he who was guiding them—but the Spirit—'Obey the Spirit', he would say between waves of song. When he deemed the moment ripe he would put his 'testing' questions.[1]

(*a*) Will every member of a Christian Church stand up ?
(*b*) Will all those who love the Lord Jesus stand up ?
(*c*) The third question was the one Jesus put to Peter, '. . . lovest thou me more than these ?'

There would be a silence then the congregation stood and sang triumphantly the hymn Diadem composed by Rev. W. C. Evans once minister at Penybryn.

'*I ganu'n llon a llafar lef—*
Mai cariad ydyw Duw'.
'To happily sing with clarion voice
That God is Love'.

and in English,—

'Bring forth the royal diadem
And crown Him Lord of all'.

The next injunction was, 'Will all who want to love the Lord Jesus stand up ?'

[1]Dr. Billy Graham's technique is very much the same—he might have learnt it from Evan Roberts.

All stand, and sing to the tune *Huddersfield* :

> ' *Duw mawr y rhyfeddodau maith* !
> *Rhyfeddol yw pob rhan o'th waith* ' ;
> ' Great God of infinite wonders
> All Thy works are miraculous '.

Other hymns followed, until the whole congregation had been subjected to a spiritual sauna—it was sound not sense that converted. There were individuals who withstood the Revival such as Gildas Rees who felt that ' the fervour and excitement around him were unnecessary adjuncts to the simple communion between a man and his God '.[1] There is considerable blackmail in the exhortation to stand up and be counted. That is why trade unions object to the secret ballot—which would shelter those weak in moral courage. I have heard Dr. Billy Graham professionally ruthless, putting the pressure on the reluctant in his congregation, and I have always felt it was most unfair, and certainly not as bluntly honest as the bus driver who dropped his passengers at one of Billy Graham's meetings with the parting words, ' There will be no time for you to be saved tonight for the bus will leave here at 9 o'clock sharp '. They all caught the bus ; Salvation like Godot, was for another day. Among the Nonconformists it was believed that God through the Revival was setting the stamp of his approval on them and on the Liberals. The Rev. Elvet Lewis announced that the Welsh nation had been summoned ' by the Providence of God to stand before the civilised world, to declare that they were going to get rid of priestcraft in every form. He thought it was a happy combination that the revival and revolt should synchronise, and be part of the same spiritual and practical movement. The fanatics produced by the Revival would forbid the young men their rugby football and cricket, their concerts and eisteddfodau, their pubs and clubs, their reading of novels and of newspapers. They called for a Samuel to lead the erring souls back to the Sunday School, to the dewy delights of the Prayer Meeting or the Bible Society. But the euphoria generated by the mass hysteria gradually wore away, and the nation became itself again. As Housman said,—

> Oh, when I was in love with you,
> Then I was clean and brave,
> And miles around the wonder grew
> How well I did behave.

---

[1]*Queen of the Rushes*. Allen Raine. p. 132.

And now the fancy passes by,
And nothing will remain,
And miles around they'll say that I
Am quite myself again.

The desire for a thorough soaking in a spiritual bath receded but it did not entirely disappear. The 'saints' still hoped that another mass stirring of the spirit would come—just as in ancient times, the faithful believed that King Arthur would return. Throughout the history of mankind, Messiahs, prophets or 'con-men', have never had much difficulty in persuading the masses to accept them, and to believe in their message, at least for a while. The ministers who were the professionals, rather liked their flocks to have been 'revivalised', for they were then anaesthetised, and could be operated upon ; there was always hope that some of the conversions could be made permanent.

The minister who baptised me in the muddy brook Pille was the Rev. John Thomas, who took charge of our two chapels in 1908, and stayed till 1927. He was a good man—with a very strong personality, and a first-class brain. He was over-endowed with love of religious austerity ; to him religion had to have discomfort in it to be thoroughly acceptable. He was a natural 'teacher', and his sermons were mostly expositions, followed by exhortations. He revived the Young People's Society which flourished mightily, meeting every alternate Thursday at 8.15 p.m. At this moment, I am looking at the programme for Session 1912/13 and it is formidable. For instance what a night it must have been when these three papers were read : (i) *History of the Jews* ; (ii) *The Influence of Bad Company* ; (iii) *Resurrection* ; while on an evening in March, Frances Michael edified the company with a paper entitled *The best way to start another religious revival.* Later programmes show that there had been a movement away from the pompous and ponderous ; instead there were happy little chats about *Twm o'r Nant ; George Grenfell ; Hiraethog ; Samuel Coleridge Taylor ; William Carey ; Old Welsh Folk Songs ; The Welsh Bible ; John Bunyan ; William Cowper ; Elizabeth Fry.* Throughout each session there would be a Social, a Concert, a 'Penny Reading' and an Eisteddfod. It was at these *Eisteddfodau* that I became the Great Lover. I never submitted less than fourteen closely written pages for the *Best Love Letter* competition. My sweetheart was called Thora, for at that time I thought it was a lovely name, first heard by me when Benchi Lewis sang in his lovely tenor voice the song so-called—'Speak to me Thora, etc.'

Well, I spoke to her in my love-letter in burning words of passionate adoration, swearing vows of eternal fidelity—the whole works—it was fun—more boys should practise the art. Of course the winner had to go on the stage to be awarded the prize, and the adjudicator missed no opportunity to do a bit of ragging—' Here you are girls—if he is half as good as his letter—get him to take you home tonight, etc., etc. ! ' Then the prettiest girl present would be asked to place the bag with the prize in it, round my neck amid delighted shouts of ' a Kiss, a Kiss ', ' *Cusanwch hi* ', ' Kiss her '—and so with flaming faces we'd have a go, only to make an absolute self-conscious ' bosh ' of it. Another popular competition was the impromptu speech and the six unknown questions. In the impromptu speech you gained marks for being funny. Once I was asked to speak for 3 minutes about a *Pig* so I began, ' A pig is a square animal with a leg on each corner '. It brought that unsophisticated house down; after all we were simple folk. There would always be a catch question such as, ' What was the name of the father of the sons of Zebedee ? ' or ' Brothers and sisters have I none, but that man's father is my father's son '. What is the relationship ? In the instrumental competition there was quite a selection. I always used a concertina, but I never won, for Andrew was too good a player and musician on almost any instrument. It was he who first introduced the delightfully flutey toned porcelain ocarina to us. That boy could perform creditably on the organ, piano, violin, recorder, mouth-organ, flute, ocarina, accordion, concertina, penny-whistle, in fact he was a ' natural '—and has well earned the musical honours which later were bestowed upon him.

The time came when we were of an age to be immersed, which varied from fifteen to eighteen. One Thursday the minister arrived ten minutes early at the Young People's Society, intending to talk to us about baptism. Only those who had been immersed could take communion, and the strict Welsh Baptists would share communion only with others of similar beliefs. On asking where the boys were, the minister was told that we were all in one of the fields nearby, so he came along. What we were doing was assisting a big dog named *Gelert* belonging to Ralph, to have intercourse with a much smaller pedigree bitch belonging to one of the other boys. Both dogs were terribly willing and grateful, so we upturned a box and stood the sacrificial lady on it. Before anything could happen, we spied the minister and ran away. When the question of baptism was broached to me later that evening at the meeting, I stalled, saying it was a very serious step to take, and that I wished to ponder on it. That was all right, for the minister promised to pray for us, and also the deacons and the brotherhood,—an array of regular troops whose intercession he felt sure would bring about the desired decision. In those days the Baptists preferred the Old Testament to the New, and like the evangelist Evan Roberts, they believed in a personal God, One who was a dispenser of discipline, One who punished because He loved, the sort of God who taught Moses those conjuring tricks which so impressed Pharaoh. They believed that the hand of God could be on them, their animals, their crops ; a drought could be interpreted as a punishment for some backsliding of which they had been guilty. Prosperity depended on the maintenance of good relations with this Old Testament God. A story I heard many a time concerned a farmer who decided to do some haymaking on a Sabbath, lest his harvest be spoilt. No sooner had he and his sons begun to toss the hay about, than there was a very loud thunder-clap, at which the farmer yelled, ' It's no good boys, He has seen us. Let's get back to the house '. Maybe after that, he believed in the God who could create a grievous murrain, a plague of boils and blains, or of frogs, lice, and flies. Like Job they felt that the average man that is born of woman was full of trouble. When the minister was taking the evening service at the sister chapel, four members would conduct a prayer meeting at ours. Their prayers were impromptu, and were uttered as they knelt by the big seat, *seddfawr*, where the deacons sat. Often their utterances would savour of neurotic self-abasement,—' O Lord, I am as dust, and unworthy to approach Thy glorious throne of grace, but I am desperate—and without Thee I am a lost soul doomed to damnation. Throw out to us O Father in Heaven the life-ropes of Thy promises and haul us into Thy ship of salvation. Turn not Thy face away from us now while the waves are waxing fiercer and our strength waning, etc., etc.' Pious decent-living folk would tell God that they were such sinners that in themselves they did not deserve salvation, but only as an act of grace and favour and if it were His will. They prayed as if their souls were heavily laden with guilt ; they grovelled sycophantically before this unpredictable God capable of great wrath. Many, no doubt were in a genuine state of spiritual unease, believing that their secret thoughts and sins were known, even catalogued by God the Father, in a huge ledger book in Heaven. They believed in a final accounting,—in the *dies irae*. Therefore they relentlessly immolated their human dignity, and constantly marred their inward peace. There were some few, like my grandfather James, a genial agnostic, who were not troubled. He used to say that there was enough religion and to spare, so long as his wife Hannah was around. She was a fervent strict Baptist who believed in the literal truth of the Holy Book. She used to say—' Every word of it is true for it is the work of the Lord '. She would have been shocked at the liberties taken by recent translators of the Bible.

After some months the minister returned to the subject of my baptism. Again I held out much to my mother's annoyance, for she felt it was bad manners to go against the minister. I argued that *immersion* could not possibly matter that much—what about Church christenings, or the Methodist token wetting of the forehead ? I was not popular—the deacons redoubled the intensity of their prayers, for I was now definitely on the danger list—I was a soul to be saved at all costs. Finally the summer before I went to the War, when expectation of life at the front was down to about three weeks,—I capitulated—just to please my mother, and the minister who was a very pleasant, sincere person. Preparations were made for the ceremony which was to take place at 10 a.m. on a Sunday. The river was dammed by means of a sluice, and any floating rubbish skimmed. Upstream the cows stood in the cool shady shallows to escape the warble fly, muddying the stream with their feet and in other ways. The adjoining farm house served as a changing room.

The ceremony at the baptistry usually began with a talk on the history of baptism, with John the Baptist immersing Christ in the River Jordan, and a statement about the efficacy of baptism by immersion in saving souls. The implication was that only those baptised like Jesus had any real hope of salvation. A prayer for those about to be dipped followed, with many ' Amens ' from the deacons and some others who were unduly moved by the occasion. The candidates were lined up by the pool, in the order they were to go in. The minister was clad in a suit of waders reaching to his wrists and his neck. The senior deacon handed each of the candidates down the three steps after which the minister would take them to the deep end saying,—' I am baptising thee my Son, or Sister, in the Name of the Father, Son, and Holy Ghost, Amen ! ' Down went the victim, up came the feet and legs, but the decencies were preserved for the white dresses of the girls had pieces of lead sewn into the bottom hem, except of course that as there were no bras in those days the blouses clung to their nubile breasts, no doubt much to the secret delight of the holy ones gathered around. Some would swallow a few mouthfuls of the water and while they spluttered and gasped, the crowd would chant, '*Diolch Iddo, diolch Iddo, diolch Iddo, byth am gofio llwch y llawr*', 'Thanks to Him, Thanks to Him, Thanks to Him for always remembering the dust of the floor!' This covered the emergence of one, and the entry of another into the pool. There was a story told about a very absent-minded old minister who immersed his candidates three times, once after Father, another after Son, and a third time after Holy Ghost! When all the prepared candidates had been dipped, a general invitation was issued for anybody who wished to be saved, to come in and be baptised. I remember an eloquent old preacher who had practically hypnotised his audience, receiving as many as six volunteers, who stripping off their jackets appeared to be in a state of high religious exhilaration as they pushed blindly into the pool to receive their immediate immersion and instant salvation. Later on some of them would be feeling like eunuchs as they remembered the hearty life which they had lived before conversion prohibited further indulgence in it. I never liked this tampering with the freedom of choice of these simple folk. There was current after the great Revival of Evan Roberts, a pleasing anecdote about two colliers who worked a small level on a Welsh hillside. Both had been converted and immersed. They kept a goat to supply them with milk. Said Dai, 'Twm it isn't fair is it for the old goat not to share our salvation through baptism. Let's baptise her'. So they dammed the mountain stream, and Twm led the Nanny to Dai who was standing in the pool ready to immerse it. The goat, which was an extremely intelligent creature, had other ideas and butted Twm head over heels into the water, from which he emerged spluttering maledictions on the cause of his plight. Then he shouted, 'O dammo Dai, christen the bastard, and let her go to Hell'.

There is something terribly intolerant in religion. Most horrible things have been perpetrated in its name. Most of those Baptists who so enjoyed the spectacle of baptism by immersion would have had ancestors who would have gone to see a Catholic being hanged, drawn and quartered, or watched while a crazy old biddy was being tortured and burnt as a witch. Their alibi would have been respectable, for in the 22nd chapter of Exodus they were told, 'Thou shalt not suffer a witch to live'. The result of this Biblical command was that between 1640 and 1660, over 4000 persons suffered for witchcraft in England, Wales and Scotland. Puritan Suffolk was notorious for its witch hunts. Pious divines like Calamy and Fairclough, had no hesitation in serving as judges in the case of

Rev. John Lowes, Vicar of Brandeston, and condemning him after torture, when he was in his eightieth year. Even the famous Dr. Thomas Browne, author of *Religio Medici*, stated at the trial of the witches at Bury St. Edmunds in 1664, that in his opinion, the three women on trial were indeed witches. By comparison Wales has a good record and has not indulged in witch-hunting to any great extent. Perhaps they did not believe so much in the supernatural powers of witches, as in a jealous God, who might bring sickness, famine, disease in cattle, or blight on corn.

When I look back to those who people my childhood memories, I am amazed anew at their cheerfulness, kindness, hospitality, and uncritical faith. In the midst of poverty, they could always find a crust for the one worse off, a helping pair of hands to nurse the sick neighbour, or a cast-off clout for one of perhaps eight small children. I have always disliked hearing politicians making capital out of a recital of the poverty of their early days,—even Aneurin Bevan who was a great man, was not above it—for I have known dozens who have borne a life-time of dire poverty without complaint. One of the great fears of a family was the major operation costing say £50—which would make nonsense of a life-time's savings. Our chapel therefore had an arrangement with Swansea Hospital, to subscribe for 2 tickets annually, so that at least that number of patients could be treated for what was beyond the family's means to pay for unassisted. Sometimes a neighbouring chapel would have used up its quota—in which case we always gave up one of ours hoping that it would not be needed later by ourselves. In the midst of this poverty there was one place of relief, where the poor, the depressed, the weary, and the hearty, could relax,—the chapel. Here they heard fervent prayer, cleansing sermons, and at regular intervals a visit by one or two great preachers—whose histrionic performances must surely rank as high as those of the greatest actors of the English stage. Thus were supplied the ingredients which went into the woof and the web of the faith of the Welsh peasant. I have seen them living and dying, happy in this faith—blind faith if you like, but one that carried them through life, and as they would put it ' across the Jordan ' as well, ' their hands out-stretched in yearning for the farther shore '.[1] When I was a boy, I often listened to long intense discussions about the comparative merits of past giants of the pulpit by the connoisseurs of a good sermon, preachers like

---

[1]*Aeneid*, vi. 314.

Roberts Llwynhendy, Carmarthenshire who died in 1893, and is still a household word in this century. His eloquence was considerable. When he visited our Chapel and was in full cry in his sermon, a well-known member stood up shouting, '*Iesu mawr dyma weithio* ! ' ' Christ Almighty here's going it '. The valley of the Teify was rich in private schools and printing presses. Christmas Evans born 25 December 1766 near Llandysul, who became a very celebrated preacher, owed his early training to the Rev. David Davis of Castellhywel, Llandysul. Dafi Davis was a preacher scholar, farmer and kept a Grammar school for over 30 years. The Rev. Timothy Thomas who baptised Christmas Evans, at Aberduar, baptised over 4,000, of whom over 30 became ministers of the Gospel. There was Daniel Morris who died at Swansea in 1914, the son of a Methodist minister who insisted on baptism by immersion. He was odd, for he prayed with his eyes open but preached with them closed. Of his namesake the Rev. Dafydd Morris, Carmel, Llandebie, who was no mean performer in the sermon,—a story is told.[1] An old woman who was a regular attendant ceased to attend, the reason being lack of footwear. She had been in the habit of joining Mr. Morris in the ' hwyl '—and in a very loud voice, so he promised that he would give her a pair of new boots if she kept quiet. The bargain was struck, but as the preacher opened up in the ' hwyl ' the old lady could smell the perfume of the myrrh, aloes and caccia. When she glimpsed the purity of the Lily and the enchanting glory of the Rose of Sharon she could hold out no longer and shouted,—' Glory be—keep thy boots dear Morris, I can resist no more—Thanks ! Thanks ! ' Other giants were the Revs. Charles Davies (d. 1927), Cardiff ; E. Talfryn Jones, Seion, Llanelli, but one time of Blaenywaun, St. Dogmaels ; Aaron Morgan, Blaenffos ; John Williams, Bethania, Cardigan. Talfryn Jones was the 11th out of 12 children who left school at 9 years old after his father, a lead miner, had died, and his mother could no longer afford to pay the school fees. He started preaching in 1878, went to College—and was ordained in 1881. He was minister at Blaenywaun with 571 members and Gerasim 121. He was at Seion, Llanelli from 1900 to 1929. I heard him preach and he was indeed formidable, especially when he preached the Judgement Day sermon. He would sweat so much that the cardboard backing of his

---

[1]p. 23, *Braslun o Hanes Carmel*, Parch. Wm. Joseph Rhys, Llandyssul, 1960.

black bow tie soaked and fell away. He would take no notice of such a trifle. In his early days in 1878 he received 2/6 a Sunday for his services, but if he was lucky it could be 3/-. Other Baptist ministers of genius were Dafydd Evans (d. 1866), Ffynnonhenry; Tom Phillips (d. 1936), Bloomsbury, London, and Benjamin Thomas (d. 1893), Newcastle Emlyn. Phillips was bred at Rhydwilym, so was well known in our district. I heard him preach several times. Charles Davies of Cardiff a saintly type of preacher was much in demand at the big meetings or Sessions. People would walk great distances to listen to these men preaching. Their meetings were so crowded that they had to be held in the open air—and this without the aid of microphones. Three sessions on Sunday by as many as seven top-class performers whose piety could not oust the jealousy they felt for each other. It was a competition for the place of ' top-dog ', and every artifice, every histrionic trick, were employed. Each one preached for over an hour, less would disqualify. It was terrific stuff, and I enjoyed it immensely. Perhaps these giants were not as honest as their brethren of to-day, but they filled their chapels to overflowing, while our modern preachers preside over an ever diminishing congregation.

I remember how William Breit, an old man who earned his living hauling with a little donkey cart, walked in his clogs at night to Fishguard from Cilgerran, a distance of 20 miles, stayed for the 10 a.m., 2 p.m. and 6 p.m. services, to listen to a total of six or seven sermons, then walked back on Sunday night discussing the merits of each sermon with his fellow travellers. The nearest comparison to this knowledgeable discussion of a sermon is a crowd of Welshmen in a pub discussing an international rugger match they have witnessed, or a few nostalgic old men talking about Percy Bush or Bancroft—the very persons who would switch later that evening to a talk beginning, ' I remember hearing Roberts Llwynhendy at So and So, preaching on the Judgement to come, etc.' It is no disrespect to mix rugger with sermons in Wales—they are both most respectable Welsh passions. There were two brothers in North Pembrokeshire, Glasnant and Jubilee Young, both preachers of considerable power. I would travel quite a distance to listen to a sermon by some-one of the calibre of Jubilee Young. His melodious voice in the ' hwyl ' was cumulative magic ; he was a wonderful performer, and a great showman. In his day he was the Garrick of the Welsh Baptist circuit, a polished practitioner of the ancient art of oratory. His audiences knew their Bible, and he was preaching to congregations willing, even fervently desiring to be moved, to be hypnotised, to be laid spiritually. At a certain moment, his sense of timing impeccable, he would subtly modulate his voice, and there he was embarking on the ' hwyl '. The voice changed to a sing-song tone, the delivery became cadenced, and the content of the sermon assumed harmonious poetic periods, free-ranging, but highly charged with emotion. Preacher and congregation became possessed, and the mouth of the preacher was now a trumpet whence issued ecstasy ; it had become the instrument sounding not the voice of Jubilee Young but the authentic voice of God speaking to his chosen people. It was the voice of a Father who was angry, forgiving, loving, kind, an understanding Father who rewarded repentance with salvation, with an everlasting life among the saints. The anguish endured by the preacher was evident to all, for the veins of his neck and temples stood out, while streamlets of sweat made furrows down his face. His collar and tie became sodden proof that he was wrestling mightily on their behalf. He was on a ' hot ' line to God. Then, when the climax, or the pinnacle of the ' hwyl ' had been reached there was a *rallentando*, a coasting down from the climax to the relaxed tempo of normal life, a steady descent from the high mountain peak in the rarefied air, to the plain below. Throughout the sixty to seventy-five minutes of the sermon the congregation had suspended all judgement, abandoned all doubts. Blasted with ecstasy they were indulging in an ' affaire ' with God. This fiskery of the spirit was most joyful, and it was legitimate. When it ended, the congregation awoke out of their trance and felt cleansed. Men like Jubilee Young or Roberts, Llwynhendy, were the folk heroes of Wales, who created the Welsh Nonconformist Conscience, and then became its custodians.

In politics, they were as we all were, Liberals. Of the pictures hanging in our house, a pride of place was accorded to those of Gladstone, Lloyd George and Christmas Evans. Lloyd George was the Jubilee Young of politics. His voice was pure seduction, or impure ; it depended on your point of view. I have witnessed a hostile audience with thought of lynching in their minds, making the tactical mistake of letting Lloyd George speak first, and before they were aware of it they had been seduced by the magic of his personality of which that wonderful voice of his was a dominant part. And of course, he was very good-looking. We must not be too critical of the characters of these preachers nor ungenerous to their memory. They kept the people sane, and the fear of God prevented many from doing what they otherwise would have done. Once a week at least they supplied to a hungry people a panoramic glimpse of the Promised Land. Sermons were often package-tours of the Holy Land, conducted personally by the minister. Together they would go to the top of Pisgah, ascend Mount Sinai in the steps of Moses, taste and spit out the bitter waters of Marah, and emerging from the Old into the New Testament they would refresh themselves with a draught of deep-cooled water from Jacob's well outside Samaria, and remember the woman with whom Jesus discussed His gift of water which cured thirst for ever. And they did it on a shoe-string salary. Christmas Evans received £17 a year for all his pastoral work in the early 19th century. Nearer our time in 1933, our Chapel's share of the minister's stipend, was £78 only, which rose to £148.4.0 by 1950. The fees charged for professional attendance to one's salvation were indeed modest.

When the minister was absent through any reason we usually had a *supply*, and these preachers were not considered to be in the top flight, for they were amateurs rather than professionals ; good simple souls, who often had other jobs to do as well. I remember one such exhibiting much skill and artistry in the way he knocked up a sermon as if he were making an omelette. He hitched it to the whole life story of Job, which he obviously knew by heart.

First there was the dramatic setting of the scene ; Satan taunting the Lord God for his faith in the goodness of Job, by suggesting that if God were only to touch all that Job had, Job would soon curse him to his face. God therefore agreed to let Satan test Job, and the bet was on. Satan smote Job with sore boils from the sole of his foot unto his crown, and he had to sit among the ashes, scraping himself with pieces of broken pottery, and the preacher went on something like this,—' Beloved people, think of the anguish of it all,—with boils on his feet, on his legs, on his thighs ',—we now waited with bated breath for the next anatomical location to be affected ; ' boils on his chest, several on his back, and his neck was covered with the biggest boils of all '. This was a shrewd move. The horny sons of the soil who had all suffered from carbuncles in their time, would surreptitiously move a hand to the place on their necks where once crops of carbuncles had flourished, the painful memory of which the sermon in progress had revived. Having established beyond all doubt the intense suffering of Job, the preacher then proceeded to string a garland of quotations from the later chapters, where God is busy cutting Job down to size. The beauty of the prose became apparent as he read, especially the description of the glory of the horse which was much appreciated by those who worked daily with that noble creature. Finally Job submits unconditionally, and God blessed ' the latter end of Job more than his beginning : for he had fourteen thousand sheep, and six thousand camels, and a thousand yoke of oxen, and a thousand she-asses '. ' My friends hesitate not to submit to God for He will be generous ', and here there was a hint, that He blessed those who obeyed Him, not only in a spiritual sense, but also materially ; in crude words—it might very well be good business ! And after all this, did not Job live for 140 years, blest by seven sons and three beautiful daughters ? Again the preacher emphasises the rewards to those who humbly submit to the Lord, in all weathers, in all places, in sickness or in health, in prosperity or in tribulation, remembering always that He deserted not his servant Job.

All preachers have been substantially assisted in their work by the incomparable beauty of parts of the Bible. When I was a boy we were given chapters from the Bible to learn by rote. We all learnt ' Remember now thy Creator in the days of thy youth . . .' Although mostly incomprehensible to me at that age, its tragic beauty was almost overwhelming. I felt that the end of the road had come for some people somewhere—a major calamity had struck—perhaps plague which had left the survivors with nothing more to do than to remember their Creator ' because man goeth to his long home, and the mourners go about the streets. Or ever the silver cord be loosed, or the golden bowl be broken, or the pitcher be broken at the fountain, or the wheel broken at the cistern '.

The route to the pulpit from the farm, the quarry or the mine in the old days was via the Prep. Schools, of which there were many in the 18th and 19th century—but in my day a candidate for the ministry had first to be examined by three experienced ministers to ascertain whether the ' call ' was genuine ' after all work at the coal face or on the farm was much harder than the work in the pulpit, and also far less glamourous. There was the attraction of the black suit of a minister with a frock coat, silk facings and a top-hat, and he was *persona-grata* everywhere. When he ate abroad only the very best would do, and he would return from an away engagement laden with gifts of food. Then there was the lure of the power an eloquent preacher wielded in the pulpit. This perhaps was the greatest attraction of all. If the candidate was deemed satisfactory he would be sent to a Baptist College, of which there were several in Wales,—at Haverfordwest, Pontypool, Cardiff and Bangor. The family, the Chapel, and the Baptist Association would help the student through his college till he was deemed ready for a *call* to a pastorate. For some the choice of career was thoroughly worldly—to have charge of a chapel, to develop the *hwyl* and perhaps please the richer, the more influential members of their congregation. These I believe were in the minority ; most ministers were God-fearing, good decent men, who regarded themselves as ' fishers of men ', savers of souls. Many of them won bardic honours, often the coveted crown or chair at the National Eisteddfod. Success of this nature greatly increased their popular appeal. To be an eloquent preacher, and a chaired bard as well, was an additional source of influence over the laity, for in Wales poetic utterance is a powerful source of seduction. It was in the thirties on a fine Sunday morning that one such appeared at my mother's house high up on the hill in St. Dogmaels. He was the Rev. Dewi Emrys James, (1881—1952) already a legendary figure. As he clomped towards us he was singing and declaiming verse. He was invited in at once, for Mother was completely spell-bound by him. He ate an excellent breakfast of bacon and eggs, and later took some wine. He talked and recited poetry, including *Pwllderi*, which was his winning composition at the 1926 National Eisteddfod. This had a special appeal for us, as it is written in the dialect of North Pembrokeshire. Poor Dewi Emrys ; he had many failings, and the Establishment were inclined to withdraw their skirts from him, but the people loved him for he was a Bard and they reverenced him as such. In the afternoon our honoured guest departed down the steep hill, a shuffling shabby figure wending his way to another night's lodging and hospitality where the halo of his bardic crown would glow comfortingly while he held forth to an appreciative audience. As soon as he had disappeared from our sight, my wife composed this stanza to the wandering bard she had just met for the first time.

The Clerwr[1]

You are old now, and no longer very clean,
Yet your poor feet find the old ways
By hedgerow briar and round the steep corners
Of simple villages you used to know
When you perhaps were simple too
And innocent of guile.
And your old lips, too sullied now for kissing,

---

[1]Published in *The Welsh Review*, July 1939.

Remember still the songs they used to sing
At haymaking ; so blithely now and careless
You shamble down the hill,
Singing to the glory of the morning
The sunlight and birds. And then because
The imperishable brain has still its cunning
You add a verse of purest poetry
Brilliantly twisted, that cries out in proof—
The spirit is the same,
The body, traitor—to youth.

As a small boy I had to help finish on a Saturday the tasks which were not to be done on the Sunday. Chapel folk knew that a man was blessed who kept the Sabbath day. The numerous exhortations in the Bible in connexion with the Sabbath were well-known, and most of the people could quote them. Therefore all boots and shoes had to be cleaned before Saturday midnight, all vegetables prepared, culm mixed, and firewood cut, enough hay and other food for the animals brought in—all laundry work—the never-ending starching and ironing had to be completed on Friday or Saturday, and a supply of water fetched from the well. What a tedious task boot-cleaning was. First of all there were soft bars of Berry's blacking to be mixed with water in an Oxford marmalade pot, mud to be removed from the footwear—then an application of this dreadful black viscose liquid. Finally a long session of hard brushing before even a glimmer of shine would reluctantly appear on a toecap, which is the most susceptible part of a boot's anatomy. I seem to remember that Dickens somewhere mentions this beastly unaccommodating so-called boot-polish.

I am referring only to the period before the First World War. This war drastically changed people's attitude to the observance of the Sabbath, but before 1914 there were still some who would hang a cat on a Monday for killing of a mouse on a Sunday.[1] My parents held that the Sabbath was made for man, and not man for the Sabbath, so we children became more and more exempt from doing dull chores on Saturdays. Gradually we led perfectly natural lives on the Sabbath, in no way stilted by a load of hypocrisy.

---

[1]R. Brathwaite, *Barnabee's Journal*, Part 1.

POPPIT

When it is Mid-Lent in England boys and girls proclaim with thumping gusto that, ' It is the day of all the year, Of all the year the one day '. It is Mothering Sunday, a day not celebrated in Wales. Neither did we sing many carols at Christmas, except those which did duty as hymns as well, like ' While shepherds watched their flocks by night '. For us the day of all the year was the annual Sunday School outing to Poppit—always Poppit, because there was not a better place, a perfect paradise for children, safe for bathing, with glorious sands and rocks. Penybryn Baptist Sunday School first went officially to Poppit in 1881, and on that occasion John Jenkins y Wagen transported the children in the waggon which he used to carry luggage from Crymmych then the railway terminus, to Cardigan. Carts carried the adults, a practice which persisted until after the First World War. The Board School at Bridell was always shut on this day.

In summer, usually in July, August or September, the whole of the Sunday School resolved itself into a Committee, and the date of the proposed outing was decided. Dates already fixed by other chapels were avoided ; due regard was paid to the likely end of the late hay harvests, for nobody was to miss the great treat because their hay was still ungathered. In 1906 the hay harvest was so late owing to heavy rains, that the trip to Poppit did not take place till 6 September. The day having been fixed, collectors were appointed and allocated to districts. They worked in pairs. I remember on one occasion calling at a farm run by a widow, to collect her donation towards the seaside-trip. She was most hospitable and for a *doch-an-dorris* gave us each a tumblerful of one of her home-brewed wines. Its effect upon us was speedy and comic. We could not stop laughing, and were excessively witty—or so we thought. Neither of us succeeded in mounting our bicycles without falling off immediately—and the hospitable lady ? she was leaning over the wall of the court by the front door helpless with laughter. They were good wholesome times. When we had completed our round we would add up the entries in our little note-book, and compare the total with the cash in our pockets. It never tallied, and we had to make good the deficit out of our own pocket money. A sub-committee of ladies decided on what arrangements were to be made for feeding the multitude. Barons of best beef were bought, and several small American hams. There was 'shop' bread, and the attractive big loaves of home-baked bread, both white and brown, home-made cakes, plain and fruit, and the various vegetables like new potatoes and broad beans. Bananas, oranges and sweets were bought from the proprietor of the local shop, who was a senior deacon of the chapel. Ample fuel for the cooking fire was taken down early in the morning with the food. After the hams had been cooked they were dressed with Demerara sugar, and left to cool.

The food was eaten in a long low shanty owned by Dinah and her husband the Captain. Inside were four long tables, the two farther from the door being set on a terrace a foot above the others. Light was shed on them by skylights fixed in the roof. Dinah charged a fee for the use of the shanty, all cutlery, plates, boilers, tumblers, tea cups. She also provided the long white table cloths. The use of the nine-pin skittle-alley was included in the hire charge for the day. Small boys were given a penny to lift the huge wooden ball into the trough which returned it to the players. The sporty gents would have the odd wager or two on the players of their fancy. I noticed that my father was always backed, for he was known to be a 'natural' at any game of skill.

The night before the great and glorious day, we children could hardly sleep but kept on pestering our parents, by asking whether it was time to get up. At last the all-clear for action was given, and we collected our gear for the day. My sisters took their buckets, spades and a box to contain the shells they were intent on collecting. When the living creatures inside the shells had died, emitting the veritable stink of corruption in so doing, and having their revenge on those who brought them away from the sea, the shells would be used in the game of dandies. We boys would have our lengths of gut and various hooks to catch the rock-fish and crabs. Most families had junior members who brought a pair of butterfly swimming wings to assist their natatory progress. Only big boys used cotton bathing drawers which were so thin, that they were only token briefs, but what could one expect for a price of less than a shilling.

The rendezvous was always on the village crossroads opposite the chapel, and the order was to be there at half-past seven. There were one or two, who year after year were always late, and one cart was kept behind to pick up these stragglers. What a day for the carters ! They had freshly painted the carts, spent hours grooming the horses and had gaily decorated their tails and manes with coloured ribbon with corn-dollies on their foreheads. They themselves were clad in breeches with impeccable black shining leggings and boots. There was considerable rivalry between the various équipes, much of it expressed in broad badinage mingled with loud guffaws. If there was a drizzle early in the morning the wise men would pronounce gnomically that it was only a ' shower before the tide '—it would be lovely later, more often than not it was. Nothing was said or done that could possibly reduce the buoyancy of the occasion. I do not remember ever seeing a four-wheeled waggon—for the simple reason nobody used them in our part of Wales—apart from the carriers. Brakes or waggonettes could have been hired, but no, this was a proud do-it-yourself occasion, so carts it was—clean—with the axle tree greased, and to accommodate the load a *treble* was fixed on each cart—and on the treble sheaves of corn on which the passengers sat. The more crowded a cart was, the better. I have an old photograph of one of these trips and about 150 people in all can be counted. The minister, his wife and family would be transported in a gig or governess trap—out of respect for the cloth—but as their children grew up, they would gravitate to the carts where they could sit squeezed tight against their boy or girl friend. By about 8 a.m. the superintendent of the Sunday School gave the order to move off —except the cart remaining to pick up the stragglers, and the triumphant 4 miles progress to the sea began. Various hymns were sung ; flippant greetings exchanged with all the people *en route* who came out of their houses and waved to each cart-load as it passed. The real singing was to be heard on the return journey in the gloaming. On arrival the carts were unloaded, the likely lads making much of their opportunity in helping the pretty girls down. There were coy blushes indicating some advance in their affairs—the silent language of pressure, pats and hugs being well understood and applied by all involved. The horses were taken out of the shafts, and there was much competition among the boys to be allowed to ride them to the stabling provided at the neighbouring farms. The ladies by this time had donned whiter than white aprons, and were calling us all to light refreshments—pop in those lovely bottles sealed by a glass marble, or tea with buns and cake. After this the mad rush over the strip of shingle to the long sandy beach if the tide was out, and a collection would be made of ribbon sea-weed, shells, pebbles and other treasure trove. There were rock-fish in the pools, and caves to be explored. Our elders forbade any one to bathe when the tide was going out, quoting in support of their prohibition the dire fates of those who had disobeyed in the past. Neither were we to go into the sea until at least one hour had elapsed since the last meal. A horn and a big hand bell summoned us all to lunch, a sumptuous repast of cold ham, beef, new potatoes, cabbage, broad beans, pickles, followed by massive portions of rice puddings. Food has never tasted so good ; everyone remarking on the way sea air had revived their jaded appetites. The great event of the day was the communal dip in the sea. The ladies formed themselves into a laager to undress—great care being taken to ask someone who understood the speed of the incoming tide, where their clothes would be safe. Men were perched on neighbouring rocks in various stage of undress, pale bodies in startling contrast with their very red faces, necks and arms. None had bathing drawers, but two bandana handkerchiefs were tied together to form an *avant garde* bikini. The ladies wore no costumes, but had summer weight petticoats which ballooned as they entered the water, much to the delight of the men who made teasing comments. The ladies would reply with equal spirit, and if they found a man had strayed near them away from the ready succour of his mates, several would grab him and dip him unmercifully. What a cacophony of Rabelaisian laughter and jokes ! What a good time was had by all, with the minister remarking that his hearing had much deteriorated since the previous year ! And, bless their memory ! did they not deserve this one day after the unrelenting swink of their occupations ?

Sports were held when the tide was out, the prizes being packets of sweets—pear drops, humbugs, or three XXX peppermints. The last meal of the day was tea—gallons of it—with bananas, cake, and meat sandwiches. Again nothing was rationed. Before the start for home some of the boys and girls would sneak off in couples into the wide expanse of sand dunes. Mothers who felt their offspring were ignorant of the facts of life, and feared lest they should learn them in Dame Nature's way of trial and error in the sand-dunes, would chase after them, calling out Davi John, Ann Jane, Marged or Wynford, much to the amusement of those parents whose children as yet were too young to involve them in such agony.

When the sun was right, some time after tea, an official photograph was taken of the whole gathering. I have one in front of me at this moment, taken in 1907 or 1908. Boys and girls sitting in the front row have boots the soles of which were plastered with Blackey's steel protectors. One or two are wearing clogs, which meant that the family could not afford the price of boots. The majority of the men are wearing caps, the elder ladies big hats gaily decorated ; eight girls have floppy straw hats and long white dresses, four men wear bowlers, only one man had a boater in a mixed group of a hundred and thirty. Most women have a belt with a huge buckle to hold the blouse and skirt together, and the skirts were ankle length. Looking at the photograph again, I am astounded that our women folk today have abandoned the gorgeous hats of their grandmothers, which were kept in place by fantastic hat-pins pushed through masses of hair. And what a weapon a woman had in those long steel pins ! Even a Parisian on a De Dion Bouton bus would hesitate before playfully pinching the bottom of a lady with a hat on her head secured by four such stilettos. The return journey was better organised somehow, and all the carts started together. The horses, too were refreshed by their unaccustomed long rest. Sometimes the tide had come in to cover the roadway to a depth of about a foot, and great was the excitement as the horses splashed their way through the water. Going home through the narrow streets of St. Dogmaels the evening air, and the full tide swelling the river to its utmost width provided a sounding board for the hymns sung in harmony. Word was passed along from cart to cart giving the selection to be sung. I would love to sit again in one of those carts, and to take part in the singing of *Crugybar*, an old Welsh air, with its ineffable haunting strains, with words by the Rev. David Charles, Carmarthen, the two blending to make it the most felicitous hymn in the language. The last four lines of the last verse would be repeated many times in an unrestrained crescendo of hope and faith.

Cawn edrych ar stormydd ac ofnau,
Ac angau dychrynllyd, a'r bedd,
A ninnau'n ddihangol o'r cyrraedd,
Yn nofio mewn cariad a hedd.

In translation something is always lost, but the meaning is this,—

We shall gaze on storms and on fears
And dreadful death, and the grave,
And we safe from their menace
Wallowing in love and in peace.

On coming out into the main street, the procession would halt, and several hundreds of the local people would join us in an impromptu singing festival. It was now quite dark, but nobody carried a light. They felt they were all lit from within. Another appropriate item which was sung to lively music was *Am yr Ysgol rad Sabbothol, Clod, clod i Dduw* (For the free Sunday School, Praise, Praise to God). Other favourites were *Tôn y Botel* (Song of the Bottle), *Cwm Rhondda* (Rhondda Valley), *'Y Delyn Aur* (The Golden Harp) ; with words by the immortal William Williams of Pantycelyn ; and always *Calon Lân* (Pure of Heart), which is regarded as Wales's unofficial national anthem, sharing the pride of first favourite at international rugger matches with *Cwm Rhondda.* The tune was composed by John Hughes (1872—1914) who was born at Penybryn, in a house we called *Tŷ Tôt.* It was opposite the chapel and stood between the inn and the shop. The words to the tune were written by his friend and poet Gwyrosydd of Landore, but Asa George wrote the words for several of his other hymn tunes. I remember the house chiefly for its magnificent pot of calceolaria (fish-baskets) which filled the window facing the road. If there were any monoglot English present usually friends or relatives who lived in London, some English hymns were sung ; the ones I remember were, *Work for the night is coming* ! *Work through the morning hours* ! *Stand up, stand up for Jesus, Ye soldiers of the Cross* ; *Jesus loves me this I know, For the Bible tells me so* ; *All hail the power of Jesu's name,* to the tune *Diadem,* composed by the Rev. W. C. Evans, who had once been our minister. Of course it must not be thought that hymns only were sung ; *Cân y mochyn du,* with ribald verses rent the air, sandwiched between two solemn melodies, and I remember particularly the beauty of the rendering of *R'Hen Ffon fy Nain* (My Grandmother's Old Stick). Topical verses composed by the resident bards, *beirdd talcen slip,* would also be sung referring usually to imaginary peccadillos, feats, or love's misfortunes of the local lads and lasses. A favourite topical song was about an old character Jack y Login who often drank too much. It was sung with full dramatic effect by my friend Andrew, who was later to become a very distinguished musician teacher, soloist and conductor. The first stanza, one of several, goes something like this,—

Jac bach y Login yn y gwter mor llon
Oh Jack of the Login in the gutter so happy
Nes daeth y polisman i weiddi ' Move on '
Till the policeman came by and shouted ' Move on '
Os na r'wyt ti'n myned i rhywle siar tŷ
If thou dost not go straight home to thy house
Yn wir machgen i, gei di ddod gyda fi.
Then indeed my dear boy thou shalt come along with me.

The pleasing thing is that these verses where Jack is the butt, were composed by Jack himself.

The acknowledged leader of our Sunday School outing, was Asa George, son of the gifted Jonathan. He was a poet, politician, precentor, and deacon, a man deeply religious, who had been liberally endowed with charm and talent. I think he was related to Lloyd George, with whom he had much in common ; a taste for the ladies, tremendous charm and persuasion, a store of righteous indignation which was triggered off by any injustice to the common man, and a belief in a Liberal and Baptist democracy. People who went to Asa for help were never rejected nor despised. He was held in affectionate esteem throughout the district, and we never completed the return trip from Poppit, without singing this jingle in his honour :

See la see ba, See la see bassa,
Côr rebella (Rebecca ?) côr rebella,
Jing, jing a jingo (or Jim, Jim a Jimbo)
Asa yw y gore, y gore, y gore.

We also sang this in 1908, during the triumphant torch-light procession from Cilgerran G.W.R. station when Walter Roch, who had won the Pembrokeshire seat for the Liberals, was hauled in an open carriage to his home, *Plâs-y-Bridell.* Of course on this occasion it was Walter not Asa who was the 'greatest'. Asa died on 12 December 1948, leaving a void in our local community which was never filled. We pertinently wonder why we cannot breed his like again.

But of all the songs sung that day none had the feckless inconsequential charm of this one, which for me and many others, is still a haunting memory. I remember four verses only, but there might well have been others—

Ar lan y môr mae lilies gwynion,
At the seaside are white lilies,
Ar lan y môr mae lilies cochion,
At the seaside are red lilies,
Ar lan y môr mae nghariad innau
My sweetheart is at the seaside
Cysgu'r nos a chodi'r boreu
Sleeping nights and rising early.

Onibae ti ac onibae tithau,
But for thou and but for thee,
Buaswn i nawr lle'r own i gine,
I still would be where I was just now,
Yn yr room uwchben y gegin
In the room above the kitchen
Gyda'r ferch a'r rhuban melyn
With the girl and her yellow ribbon.

Gennyf fuwch a dau corn arian,
I have a cow with two horns of silver,
Gennyf fuwch sy'n godro'i hunan,
I have a cow that milks itself,
Gennyf fuwch sy'n llanw'r stwce,
I have a cow that fills the milk pails,
Fel mae'r môr yn taflu'i donne
As the sea throws down its waves.

Oer yw'r rhew ac oer yw'r eira,
Frost is cold and so is snow,
Oer yw'r tŷ heb tan y gaua,
Chill is the house without winter fire,
Oer yw'r eglwys heb un ffeirad,
Cold is the church without a parson,
Oer wyf innau heb fy nghariad.
Cold am I without my sweetheart.

In content these verses have much in common with early poetry, but their colloquial flavour suggests that they are not as old as they seem, unless successive generations have continuously brought them up to date. In the second verse we can sense the poet's spitting indignation, when two persons, possibly the farmer and his wife, interrupt his dalliance with the attractive maid whose bedroom was above the kitchen. ' But for you two interfering spoil-sports I would still be in the bedroom of that attractive girl with the yellow ribbon '. Then the pathos of the last verse, where the lover has lost his sweetheart, and is cold in body and miserable in spirit. What has deprived him of her sweet company ? Has he been warned to keep away from that room above the kitchen ? Hardly likely for ' courting all night ' was an accepted way of life, so we are led to the sad conclusion that she is dead, and that he who loved her is now alone and palely loitering, deaf to the song of birds, but sustained by the glorious memory of red and white lilies among which he once had fed, and of the pretty yellow ribbon which his sweetheart wore in her hair, perhaps at Poppit.

On arriving home, we would have a quick bowl of bread and milk, then bed, for we had been well-fed that day. In a few days an all-pervading smell of corruption would indicate the location of a forgotten cache of sea-shells. There followed weeks of appetising gossip *clonc* arising out of the trip, as everyone was now *au fait* with any new developments in the community, and reassessments of persons and situations were made accordingly—based on what had been seen and heard on that glorious day by the sea,—at Poppit.

VENDETTA

When I was in a junior form of the Grammar School I participated in a vendetta. Three farms, ours being one, had a right of way to the main road with carts and traps (vehicular traffic of the bureaucrat) along a rutted cartway following the hedges of two or three fields of another adjoining farm, the occupier of which had a short while previously died. He had been a good neighbour,—a kindly old Baptist deacon, well-liked by all. I do not know why, but after his death in December 1913 his wife began to question this right of way, by closing the gates with padlocked chains. Remonstances brought no redress, so one of the victims asked me to come with him to keep watch on the house of the widow, and to signal when she went into the garden, where stood the pride of the Pembrokeshire County Council—a sentry box of corrugated zinc, with a wooden seat and the appropriate hole—beneath which was a bucket. It was a pity that its designer had not studied his subject with the intelligent enthusiasm of the American Specialist whose works of art are so well described by Charles Sale,—' You see, I put a 4 by 4 that runs from the top right, straight on down five feet into the ground. That's why you never see any of my jobs upset Hallowe'en night. They might *pull* 'em out, but they'll never upset 'em '. This was the vital difference between the two designs,—the Pembroke County Council's dream-child was supplied with no means to secure it to the earth, and as the door opened inwards, this made it difficult to effect an exit when it was lying on its face. Indeed one local old boy who suffered from constipation, expired while sitting and straining in one of these, and as he was not missed for a long time his legs had stiffened like pit props against the door, and much sawing had to be done before he was extracted. The event was kept dark as far as possible, for to expire in such a place was considered unseemly. The style of one's passing was as significant as death itself, but as nobody would dare blame the Almighty publicly, the lurking thought unexpressed was that God had somehow nodded when He summoned His servant to higher service, before he could leave the privy with his dress properly adjusted, and he a pillar of the local Baptist chapel as well ! It would not have mattered so much if a Methodist or a Church of England man had been so selected.

The finest example I have ever seen of a ' small house ' was in a German garden. It was a typically Teutonic achievement in the generosity of its endowments,—spacious, airy, and the long beautifully polished mahogany seat had places for father, mother, and three children ; an example of good family planning and, with the whole family simultaneously in session, of *Deutschland uber alles.*

But I am digressing. I had been watching for about ten minutes while my confederate was hiding in the fruit bushes, when the widow came out, entered what the Arabs call the house of rest, and shut the door. I gave the signal for action. My companion was there in a flash pushing the contraption on its face, thus imprisoning the occupant in unsavoury surroundings. The angry screams were piercing, and we saw in the gloaming the cowman rushing to the rescue. Among the conspirators that night there were high hopes that the lady had been cured of her passion for padlocking gates. But alas ! no, she clearly did not consider that an upset privy with her inside it constituted an eirenicon, for she persisted, and on reflection it must be conceded that she was a woman of considerable spirit. The three aggrieved parties, my father and our two neighbours met at our house, and I listened in. When they realised that I knew of their plans—they agreed that I should come along too, and watch the house to give timely warning of anyone emerging from it. The plan devised was comprehensive, and I think rather cruel. The carts, gambo, and the trap, were housed in buildings open to the road which at this spot was a very steep hill for several hundreds of yards. These were quietly brought out, and at about two in the morning, with their shafts trailing, they were given a push to start their headlong journey down the hill until they crashed at the first sharp bend. In the stillness of the night the noise was frightening, and the last cart was on its way down when I spied a light upstairs in the house, and heard the sound of voices. I gave the alarm, and we all fled quietly homeward, wondering what the next move would be. It was amazing and unexpected—the tough old widow came to see us and said, ' I can't fight all of you. I have tried and I have failed. Let's see how we can be friends again '—and so it was, we all became friends, and a while later when she had slaughtered a naughty old billy-goat which had become rather a menace, she graciously brought us a piece of his flesh. When we had roasted, tasted and tried to masticate the meat from the body of this four-footed old roué, we wondered whether there wasn't the sound of someone laughing. I was friendly with this formidable character till she died, and afterwards with her only child, a daughter who succeeded her. My mother too became a close friend of the daughter, called on her regularly for the inevitable *clonc* and cups of tea. Neither the daughter nor her mother ever questioned me about those nocturnal happenings, a proof that they were women of some breeding. The whole affair showed that a trial of strength 'twixt stalwart folk can create mutual respect leading to a permanent friendship.

My mother was *petite*, little more than five foot in height. She had beautiful light blue eyes, which looked right into you ; they were calm, unruffled, and steady, which made it very difficult to tell a fib to her face. Nevertheless she had to laugh when she overheard the conversation between my sister and me, as we were walking through the garden towards the house on our return from a very lively party. The evening was warm and mother was sitting on a garden seat, enjoying the lovely moonlight. I asked my sister what we were going to tell mother, and she answered that it did not matter what, so long as we both said the same thing ; mother disclosed her presence by a peal of merry laughter although she knew the joke was on her. During the 2nd World War several boys from Liverpool were billeted in her home, and one of them found a pound note on the roadway. He felt that it was morally his, but mother soon disillusioned him by insisting that he take it to the Police Station there and then, saying that honesty would bring its own reward. After a month or so a policeman brought it back as as no one had claimed it, and the boy had it. He also received a commendatory lecturette with which mother improved his shining hour.

Father, on the other hand, was over six foot, well-proportioned, and good-looking. It was said that when he was young, the ladies would turn their heads to have another look at him, as he walked or rode past upon his lawful occasions.

I have never known anyone whose physical movements and reactions were so well correlated. In his youth he earned local fame as a long distance runner. His father, James, who was a master-saddler, saw to it that his sons were taught harness making, and it appears that father acquired a professional standard of skill and workmanship. They were also sent after a period on their own farm to work as labourers on large farms, to gain experience of arable as well as grassland farming. My father went to Dr. Phillips's farm, and I have heard it told many times, how the Doctor pootling around was charged by the big Hereford bull which was in the yard. He escaped into the cowshed and emerged with a pitchfork to join battle, and he succeeded in prodding some sense into the huge animal. He ordered my father to cure the creature's propensity to charge without warning, so it was agreed that after milking, when the cows and the bull with them had returned to the large pasture, father was to put in action his plan to tame the savage beast. Accompanied by the Doctor, and spare hands eager to see the fun, father armed with a seasoned ash stick walked from the hedge towards the bull who immediately charged. Father neatly side-stepping seized hold of his tail and got to work with the ash stick on his flanks, with the odd prod at the precious sensitive bag the bull carried protectively between his hind legs. Fourteen times, it was said, they went round the field till exhausted, the bull gave in, and just lay down moaning,—disgraced before all his ladies, and the young eunuchs, who no doubt rejoiced ; and it was further said, that, henceforth, it was safe for all folk to go across fields and meadows without interference from this bull. The Doctor tossed to my father a gold coin, a half-sovereign, as a reward for sportsmanship. Father was a crack shot, and I never knew him miss. He taught me how to allow for the speed of various birds and animals and gave us this advice,—' Don't point a gun at anyone unless you wish to kill him '. As a youth he had seen another lad accidentally blowing his head to pieces, when lifting a loaded gun by the muzzle from a bramble hedge. Throughout his life he observed strict discipline in connexion with fire-arms, which is absolutely necessary if accidents are to be avoided. His judgement was superb—one winter's night I accompanied him to the cowshed, and there with its eyes gleaming in the light of the hurricane lamp, was a rat sitting on the warm haunch of a cow which was lying down. Reaching gently for a stick, of which there were always several in a cowshed, he struck the rat with a lightening sweep killing it outright, but the old cow was not disturbed, and was obviously unaware of what had just taken place—for it continued nonchalantly chewing its cud.

When I first remember father, he was then working as a trainer of the horses of the local M.P.'s family, Walter Roch, a Liberal and a charming gentleman. His brother William and his mother, Mrs. Roch, were great sportsmen and also steeplechasers. I heard years later how William was trying to master a spirited raw Australian horse crossed with Arab in the exercising field, when after several falls, he turned to Father and said, 'You have a go Mort'. Father got on and yelling to Mrs. Roch to open the gate to the public road, galloped hell-bent towards the hill which stretched for almost 3 miles. As he streaked out, Mrs. Roch yelled, 'A sovereign if you stay on!' So, aided by the long steep hill, father stayed on, exhausted the fine creature, and returned with a fairly docile horse, which later was to win several steeplechases. Mrs. Roch paid her wager there and then, beaming with pleasure and appreciation, for she was in her day a notable horsewoman. William was killed in action later in Gallipoli, and Walter became the Liberal member for Pembrokeshire. He too, was a brilliant horseman and rode at least once in the Grand National. He also played cricket for Harrow when he was a schoolboy. He was born in 1880, and died in 1965. It is a matter of regret to me that I did not seek him out before he died, for he would have had much of great interest to say about the past. The best character sketch of Walter Roch is that written by a fellow member of the Reform Club, Frank Swinnerton, in his delightful book entitled *Reflections from a Village.* He relates that Roch at the Club would gaily indulge his mischievous flair for baiting and teasing. Members like H. G. Wells and Arnold Bennett were well able to look after themselves, but less brilliant members feared his darts. 'His fluency, malice, and kindness were mingled with social and political gossip, news of the commercial world, and caustic estimates of public men . . . I think Roch could have been Prime Minister if he had had the grit fully to use his natural brilliance and command the attention of the House of Commons. He made no impression there. He would not risk his own discomfiture in the virulence of debate. He could be, and was, silenced by harder, tougher, more ambitious men'. Swinnerton told me that after the second World War, Roch disappeared from the London scene, and occupied himself by managing the Llanarth estates which he had inherited, only coming to London to visit his dentist. While he was an M.P. I cannot recall Roch, or anyone else for that matter, conducting a 'surgery' to deal with local problems. Once elected the member had only to hold a few public meetings. It was a privileged existence rendered comfortable by the possession of ample independent means. The populace were proud to have returned a Liberal to Westminster, and were content to leave him alone to get on with the job of improving the lot of the common man. '*Autres temps, autres moeurs*' maybe, but a member of Parliament then, was held in high regard, whereas today he is rated as a very ordinary person. The politician no longer commands the respect his predecessor did, for the nation has had a surfeit of government, of legislation, petty regulations, sanctions, and of bureaucrats who interfere in the private lives of citizens.

My father was a superb worker in most materials especially leather or wood. He could make harness, for his father, a master saddler, had taught him. All the implements we needed in the country were made by ourselves. He showed us how to pick the right wood for the task in hand—how to make baskets and *cewyll* creels which were used to carry chaff to the animals. It was surprising how many kinds of baskets were in use—the egg basket—the shopping one, another with a lid for poultry, and various trugs for vegetables and fruit from the garden. For most implements ash was the wood used, and I believe there is none better. In winter we made rakes—some with fifteen oak tines, others with as many as twenty-five to thirty. The head was so drilled, that when the handle was split and fitted, the tines were at less than a right angle to it. If this were not done, the result was not a *sweet* rake to use. Besoms we made from birch tops cut before Christmas, which were bound by strips of bark usually willow, but oak, ash or hazel served equally well. The technique was that used by golf professionals, when they bound a wooden shafted club with waxed thread, only the strips of bark were moist and became very tight when the tapered handle usually hazel, was driven into the besom head. For use in a confined space a bundle of birch cuttings were bound without fitting a handle. Occasionally a besom was made from broom, but its wearing capacity was poor. Another winter chore which I liked very much, was to make various handles—for axes, hatchets, picks, *ceibiau* mattocks, pitchforks, bill-hooks, sickles and shovels. The Welsh *rhaw* is not strictly speaking a shovel—it has a point, and a bent handle. Bretons still use them, but the English workers I have tried to persuade to adopt it, have all declined. But there is no better tool for opening on a Good Friday the well-tilled garden soil into beautifully straight neat drills for early potatoes. I loved to make an exaggerated bend to an axe handle—I felt that here design was wed to efficiency, to make working with the tool a pleasant rhythmic passing of the time. Hammers, chisels, awls, all needed handles, and the work was done with a draw-knife, a saw, a spoke-shave, and for the final finish—pieces of glass—a broken bottle or jam pot were excellent. Then there were the treen ; the wooden *cawl* bowls, wooden spoons of various sizes to carry the broth to the mouth, the wooden scoop with serrated edge to carve curly wavelets of salted butter from a big earthenware pitcher, which stood in the dairy, the jumbo ladle called *lletwat* which had a hooked end to prevent it from falling into the boiling *cawl*, and a variety of spoons, pestles, bowls and platters. After milking, before we had a separator, the milk was left in big pans on the cool slate slabs in the dairy until the cream had come to the surface. It was then skimmed off using a large shallow wooden saucer. We nearly always worked sycamore which is such a lovely wood to shape, besides, it was freely available all around us. On rare occasions we turned pieces of cherry and apple on our old-fashioned treadle lathe. We had various types and sizes of curved carving knives all with long handles which reached the shoulder so as to obtain leverage. These were made out of old rasps or files by my uncle and cousin who were skilled iron workers. I still have scars from cuts to the finger bone, caused by inexpert use of this curved knife. What a pleasant way of spending a stormy winter evening it was, to sit by the fire, toasting bits of skimmed milk cheese, and cobbling the pungent white knotless baulks of sycamore. Father supervised our work and quietly, without fuss, demonstrated the skills involved in making each article well. The second-rate was completely unacceptable to him—he had one aim only—to achieve perfection in big or small tasks. His mansuetude was boundless, but it did not permit him to accept the second-rate. Practically every house in the *cwm* had its saw-pit where trunks of trees were sawn to the required thicknesses by two persons, one standing on top and the other in the pit. Beams, trusses, ties, boards were thus sawn and shaped *ad hoc* for the job in mind. Another intriguing ploy was to search the woods for a tree with a branch that could be used for a scythe handle—or snaith. Country bred boys walk about with their eyes open ; they love their environment and understand it. We learnt to walk quietly avoiding twigs, and at night we could feel the path through the soles of our feet. Then there was the art of staying still, not even breathing perceptibly—to see the birds and animals coming within close view. Mice, moles, snakes, ravens, wrens, weazels, rabbits, trout in the clear stream—and the heron that splendidly picturesque bird will emerge into focus if you stay absolutely still and silent. The real country is a glorious place, and in spite of its attendant hardships, it is still a privilege to be permitted to live in it.

My brothers and I had the greatest fun with a beautiful chestnut cob and a pair of evil jackasses. The cob was called *Prudence* and the conditions laid down were, that we should groom her, muck out her stall and generally see that her requirements were satisfied before ours were. We learnt how to ride bare-back, and I have ever since preferred the feel of a horse between one's legs to sitting on a saddle. Once an old *Shiekh* at *Mena House* by the Pyramids was so flabbergasted by my request to have the saddle *el cursi* removed before I rode one of his Arab stallions, that he insisted on accompanying me, to witness, I presume, my ghastly fall. But as we went along a *wadi* at full gallop he shrieked his delight, '*Wallahi ya hadritak ente ragil taib, ya sidi*'. '*By my God your honour, thou art a real lad* !' On returning to Mena he refused a fee, and promised that in future, whenever I needed a horse I should be allowed to pick the best. He was a good old sportsman, and he often rode with me—and as a sign of comradeship he would leave his own saddle behind, and remarked that as a boy in his mud village, he too rode bare-back. There's some hidden good in nearly everyone, but it is often only discovered by chance. But to return to these two donkeys. The task of catching them always developed into a miniature rodeo. Three of us would work them into the corner of the field and close in slowly upon them. Their eyes had the light of joyful wickedness with no redeeming repentance visible anywhere. Success depended on who made the first strike. How long could one delay the dart-in to seize the brutes by the ear and nostril? too long delayed, and we would be engulfed by flying hoofs (they had no shoes on) and satanic jackass laughter. There is no doubt at all that these ribald creatures enjoyed the fun—and after getting a bridle or often only a halter on, there was the further rodeo-type bucking and tight turns. The larger of the two also had the larger sense of humour. After throwing its rider, he would stop, gaze with mournful sympathy, and unutterable compassion at the prostrate figure on the ground, and wait invitingly to be remounted, when he would have thought of a few more antics. I love donkeys—they are great animals ; a real challenge. The best I ever rode were those big buck jackasses—with none of their parts removed, which are numerous in Upper Egypt. Chesterton's poem is the fruit of genius, but his picture of a Palestinian donkey is too pessimistic, too modest, too docile, and too dejected. There was a notable Methodist minister in our local town Dr. Moelwyn Hughes—a gifted scholar, whose children since have all distinguished themselves in the professions. He was a man universally looked-up to, and one day he met Bateman Bâch, a witty old character, driving his donkey and cart, from Gwbert, and he was belabouring the beast. 'Don't do that Mr. Bateman, for remember it was on the back of a donkey that our Saviour entered

Jerusalem '. ' O dammo Dr. Hughes bâch, if he had been on the back of this one, he would not have got there yet ! '

Conceit about my riding ability brought about a nasty fall when I cracked the collar-bone. Ella, the elder of the two charming daughters of our neighbour the solicitor, came down to see us on a white pony beautifully groomed, and saddled. She was older than I, but when she asked if I thought I could ride it, I accepted with alacrity, and in the excitement I did not shorten the stirrup girths. So there I was trying to ride a saddle bare back, with my short legs nowhere within reach of essential support. To show how much better I could ride than a mere girl, I switched the pony's flank sharply with a hazel rod, and we were away. I was bouncing like a cork—completely out of control, and then,—good gracious I can feel it now,—I was shot off right on to my left shoulder, and was so winded I could say nothing. It was a lesson I never forgot, but when one is young and there are charming girls to be put in their place, boys will be boys and behave in a most extraordinarily exaggerated fashion. Father was asked to clip that animal, so I went with him to turn the handle of the clipping machine. The whole performance developed into a comic show. The pony was so ticklish, that it shied and whinneyed, or giggled I should say—so finally father laid down the clippers, and dealt with the animal. It became a kind of personal wrestling match, and in a flash he had the pony flat on its side on the straw of the loose box, and he was sitting on its neck with a firm grip of its nostrils. Then he spoke severely to her, and finished his work on the ticklish areas. It occurred to me then, how primitive was this struggle between man and horse, but what a noble intelligent creature a horse is, and what a beautiful animal. I can still re-read a book like *National Velvet*, with no diminution of pleasure. Although I like motor cars as much as the next person, I would willingly trade them in for horses of all kinds. Is it too much to hope that the end of the road has not come for the glorious Suffolk Punches—the Clydesdales and our Welsh cobs. Will there always be replacement for the Royal coach-horses and the Household Cavalry. It is a good sign, when we have a Royal family which obviously adore horses. Our present Queen is never more natural and appealing, than when she has to deal with horses—she is clearly utterly at home with them, which is delightful, and I feel the horse has a doughty champion in this gracious lady.

I once read out to my father this gobbet from *Hamlet*, '. . . in form, in moving, how express and admirable ! in action how like an angel ! in apprehension how like a god ! the beauty of the world !

the paragon of animals '. I then asked him to guess the identity of the animal to which Shakespeare was referring, and without hesitation he replied, ' No doubt at all, it's a thorough-bred race-horse '.

Grandma Hannah, wife of Grandpa James the genial agnostic, was a fervent believer in the *Word.* Often when she was being worsted in an argument she would flounce out of her windsor chair, and make for the big leather covered Bible with its massive brass clasps which always stood beside the clock on the oak dresser, muttering threateningly, 'We shall now see what the *Word Y Gair,* says'. It was for her the final Court of Appeal. Here was a blind faith, which a preacher once described to our Sunday School class as follows, ' Faith is believing what you cannot see—for instance, if you were looking at a boat out in the Bay, and I told you there were two monkeys at the bottom of it but you could not see them, yet you believed my words—that is an example of faith '. Later in the public oral examination of religious knowledge held in the Chapel, the question was put to Johnny Rees—' What is faith ? ' and with an expression of ' Gosh ! this is a sitter ', he replied, ' Monkeys in a boat Sir ! ' Grandma was no better than Johnny, and she would almost suffocate us with her avalanches of moral precepts, all extracted from the *Word.* But I remember her with affection, for her genuine kindnesses, and her complete understanding of the extent of a small boy's appetite. She loved to see you coming up for second helpings. Her apple tarts were vast, being cooked on huge (and I discovered later, very valuable) willow-pattern dishes. A triangle of this delectable food, was only equalled by her suet-gooseberry or rhubarb puddings, boiled with the meat and the vegetables in a big basin with a cloth to restrain the contents from joining in the free for all.

A visit to Grandma meant renewing acquaintance with a very savage huge bitch called very appropriately *Fury.* She did not make friends easily, but she adored my father, who once, when I was in bed ill with chicken-pox, brought her home with him. I was upstairs in bed and alone in the house when I heard a growl, and there Fury was standing a few feet away from the bed, making threatening noises. If she attacked I decided to wrap a quilt around her head, and try to throw her downstairs, but first of all I tried to make friends with her—I murmured her name in a low voice, and allowed my arm to drop gently out over the side. This excited her curiosity, and stealthily approaching she sniffed it and finally—after what appeared to me an eternity—she started to lick it. When my parents returned they found us both asleep, she on the bed with a paw stretched out protectively over this helpless lad, whom she had decided in her doggy way was clearly in need of care and protection.

I also enjoyed the two annual trips to Grandma to borrow her special low slung trap which was drawn by an old pony called ' Brock ' because of its colour. This was the occasion of the picking of sugar plums and damsons of which there were several dozen trees. We all set to, to pick them when the bloom was intact, and mother would go to the local village which was no more than a long street, and sell them by the quart, a wooden bowl holding several pounds and certainly more in capacity than the quart pot. She would get about 6d for a quart, but she also had a glass mug for measuring pennyworths to children. We small boys were useful in climbing to the top of these brittle trees where the heavier adult couldn't. A tall ladder was placed very steeply against the tallest branches where, because they enjoyed most sunshine, grew the finest fruit. We used a hook to draw the farthest tips towards us. This often altered the balance and the branch on which the ladder rested would snap. We learnt by experience to stay with the ladder and if possible swing it towards a hedge or against another tree to break the fall. If there were none of these available it was a case of abandoning ship at the last moment, by making a controlled leap or vault off the ladder when it was very near the ground. If someone was at the foot of the ladder when a branch snapped it was quite easy for him to swing ladder and picker on to another part of the tree. We never considered that there was anything brave or dangerous about this occupation ; we were far more concerned lest we break the ladder than break a bone. My pal Willie and I once engaged in a painful experiment. We each claimed to have the ability to consume more plums than the other—the condition being stones and all, so we sat high up among fruit laden branches and set to, ' one for you, and one for me '. When our stomachs were distended to the limit, and we had agreed it was a draw—we parted. In the night my inside was racked with painful spasms, and I was just able to reach the safety of the ash heap, between the hen house and the piggery, when the uncontrolled, painful, and undisciplined evacuation of the plums with their twin pointed stones began. I should have mentioned that there was no ' privy ' inside the house. Sick people had to use a commode, but for the daily calls of nature, we had to use any spot that took our fancy—for there was no ' toilet ' outside either. Finally, my mother came to ascertain the cause of my prolonged absence, and was acquainted with the situation. Action followed in the shape of hot milk with chunks of bread in it. Squatting there in the light of a waning moon I combined two activities, one to get the soothing milk inside me, the other to evacuate the wretched load of plum stones. I am willing to bet that Willie and I were not unique in this kind of dare; boys hardly ever heed advice, and must find out things for themselves.

Our school was situated half-way up a steep hill, so we were often mobilised to push up the motor car of either a local lawyer or one of the local doctors. I think the lawyer had a De Dion Bouton, while the doctor was content with a Belsize. The main reason why they could not negotiate the hill without help, was lack of power, but another contributory factor was the narrow steel-studded white-walled tyres which afforded no grip when the road was wet. I thought that these machines were most beautiful—with polished brass head lamps, carbide container, radiator, and the long flexible brass tube of the horn. The passengers were always wrapped up in rugs, long scarves, and heavy overcoats, while the chauffeurs were in peaked caps and uniform. I am not sure, but I think these cars carried a Stepney—that is, a rim with inflated tube and tyre, having screw clamps to secure it to the punctured wheel. It was named from its inventor who lived at Stepney Street in Llanelli. I remember, too, one of the Bank Managers with a Triumph motor bike and side-car. Once he stopped to give me a ride, and I thought it was the most heavenly means of transport man had devised. One floated air-borne above the muddy road ; it was angelic!

Another gorgeous creature which found the hill too much for it, was the itinerary traction engine, towing its threshing machine behind. But the grimy men who managed this giant were persons of rare resource, for they fitted massive blunt steel spikes into the round holes in the huge rims of the driving wheels, which aided in this way gripped effectively and thumpingly. Our job was to collect any of these spikes which came adrift through getting stuck in the surface of the road. Two other vehicles were welcome sights when they hove on our horizon, the bright blue cockle-cart, laden with the delicious *fruit de la mer* garnered on the tide-swept beaches of south Pembrokeshire, and Carmarthenshire, and the fish cart whose driver had a stentorian voice. When he shouted *Scadan ffres*, Fresh herrings, he was heard in homesteads half a mile away. Breton fishermen can still be heard advertising their wares by calling ' *Scadan ffres* '.

THE GRAMMAR SCHOOL

When I was twelve I was informed that I was to sit the entrance examination for the local Grammar School, which had been founded as the Free School in 1653. I had no wish whatsoever to enter this School, for I had already arranged with my elder brother, who at fourteen had gone to work on the G.W.R. at Port Talbot, that he would get me an apprenticeship at a Marine Engineering Foundry in Swansea. I had read all the books about the sea that I could lay hands on, and my head was stuffed with romantic maritime dreams. I had no doubt at all that I too, would in due course take my rightful place alongside those gallant sailors who had made our country's history glorious. The Headmaster of the Board School whose record in getting any of his pupils to pass into this School was deplorable, saw in me a possible success, so I was entered. Clad in my best suit I appeared at 9 a.m. of the appointed day to sit the Entrance Exam. I was determined to play my trump card—by not answering enough to justify my selection for admission, so I answered only one question in each Section, with the foregone result that I was not admitted. It was a case of many were called, but few were chosen, and of the few I was not one.

In a twelvemonth there was another chance—when I was thirteen. This time the marine apprenticeship had come to naught, and my parents had resorted to bribery,—if I passed I should have a bicycle of my choice, custom-built to my own measurements. I ordered catalogues from every cycle maker in the Midlands, and out of my nil-experience settled on the *Quadrant Cycle Company* of Coventry which turned out to be an excellent choice. I made sure that I was well up to the standard required to pass the exam, and the result when announced was that I had been awarded a County Bursary. The bike cost £3.12.6, the bursary saved £6 tuition fees, and I received 15/10d per term to buy books. One day Mr. Cook the postman announced that my bike had arrived in a crate at the local railway station—so tingling with pleasurable excitement, I rushed off to unpack and ride it home. It was beautiful and I oiled it unnecessarily, checked that all its nuts were at the correct tension when it was apparent they were, and any other superfluous adjustments which I in my excited state could think of. As mother said, she felt I would have gone to bed with it. It was the best bike a boy could have had, and it lasted me for 3 years when I sold it for £3.10.0 to a smaller lad,—two shillings and six pence less than it had cost—helped of course by the general rise in prices during the War.

At the Grammar School I was to meet the first of the two great teachers in my life. He was Dr. Dan Rees, the Headmaster, affectionately known as *Doc.* The other I did not meet till many years later—David Nichol Smith, the Merton Professor of English at Oxford. Both were veritable Gamaliels, and both were great gentlemen. I owe to each an immeasurable debt. The opening day of Term was fine, and the only uniform required, was a school cap with the town's coat of arms on it. As I sped proudly on my new bike, I felt very much a ' new ' boy. The day opened with the roll-call in the central Hall, followed by announcements. There was no religious service—that did not become a requirement till Butler's Education Act of 1944. The School was a modern red-brick building situated at the top of the town (Pendre) and was commonly known as the County or Intermediate rather than the Grammar School. It was the product of the Intermediate Education Act of 1889. Its origins were connected with the well-known Phillips family. George Phillips of Tregibby became the owner of Cardigan Priory in 1616. His son Hector married three times, his second wife being Mrs. Katherine Fowler, the widow of a rich London merchant, and mother of the ' matchless Orinda '. When Mrs. Fowler died, Hector married as his third wife, Anne, the daughter of Sir William Wogan, of Wiston near Haverfordwest. The Wiston Wogans were very rich and owned extensive estates. In 1647 Orinda became the second wife of Hector's son James ; he then being fifty-three and she 16 years of age. They had two children, Hector who died in childhood, and Katherine born in 1656, who married Lewis Wogan of Boulston Haverfordwest, and of the fifteen children born to them only a daughter survived. The matchless Orinda died of smallpox in Fleet Street, London on the 22 June 1664, and she was buried in the church of St. Benet Sherehog, in the parish of St. Stephen's Walbrook. This church was destroyed in the Great Fire, and it was not rebuilt. When Orinda died her tremendous contemporary fame as a poet died too. James Phillips's third wife was Jane, daughter of Sir R. Rudd, whose seat was at Aberglasney, Carmarthenshire. We have in these marriages an example of the important part they played in the accumulation of wealth and land. A rich widow was just as good 'negotiable currency' as an heiress. The Phillipses had the reputation of being grasping, but in 1647 when he married Orinda James Phillips went around the borough of Cardigan petitioning for money to found a Free Grammar School. 'Free' meant that the School was independent, and the Borough Council who administered it were *free* to charge appropriate fees. James Philipps stated in his petition that there was no school within 40 miles, and that only the best class of gentry received any education at all, and that 'preaching does not at all edify them'. In 1653, the Free Grammar School was officially founded, the livings of Llansantffraed (4½m. N.E. of Aberayron) and Lampeter being sequestrated for its support. At the Restoration in 1660 the livings were returned. The Borough Council passed *inter alia.*—'That in case the parrents of schollars cannot afford for their children's dyett in any inn or alehouse within this Towne, then the Mayor and Councell or the major part of them doe seeke a place convenient and the rate. (2) That such poore schollers as shall be recommended by the Mayor and Councell of the Schoole shall be admitted free and provision, both of apparell and meate shall be made for them out of the Treasury accordinge to their quality and condition'.

James Philipps was a Colonel in the Parliamentary Army, and he and his brother Hector were enthusiastic hunters of Royalists. It was James who presented the two silver maces to the Corporation of Cardigan, each bearing the Royal arms with the letters 'C' and 'R' on either side. The silver handle of the larger has this inscription—*Domum Armigeri Jacobi Phillipps de Tregibby, in Comitatu Cardigan Armigeri Dedit burgo Cardigan An domi 1647*'.

Looking back at my Grammar school days, I realise anew that it was a very good school. It was a happy school as all co-ed establishments tend to be, with the Staff nearly all competent teachers. The emphasis was upon learning, and the whole *ethos* of the system stemmed from the character of its great Headmaster, Dr. Dan Rees —but more of him later. On that first day I was placed in Form 2, given a list of books we were to buy, and issued with several exercise books, and one red board-cover notebook for writing up our experiments in Chemistry. We were 30 pupils in that Form—girls and boys being equally divided. Lesson periods were only 25 minutes in duration and the subjects we had to study that first year were,—Welsh, Latin, French, German, English Language, but no formal Literature till we had acquired a real grounding in Language, English Composition, History, Arithmetic, Algebra, Geometry, Chemistry, Geography, and Geometrical Drawing. Physics was not a subject considered important enough to be taught. I have never had a single lesson in it ; perhaps I'm all the better for that ! I soon became aware of my inherent likes and dislikes. I liked best of all, and in this order, Latin, Chemistry, Literature, History, Geometry. I disliked Algebra, German, and the technical part of English Language—especially the passages set for parsing and analysis from a book modestly entitled by its author, Mr. Alfred West,—*The Elements of English Grammar*. It lasted us throughout our stay at school. It left an indelible impression, for to this day I can distinguish between Noun, Adverb, and Adjective Clauses ; Compound and Complex sentences still have a meaning ; I have not forgotten that the simple family of Pronouns can be classified as Personal, Demonstrative, Reflexive, Relative, Interrogative, Indefinite, Distributive, and Possessive ; and that Adverbs failed to remain immune from a tidy mind which distinguished them as of Time, Place, Degree, Manner, Certainty and Reason, and Consequence. In due course we became adepts at performing the most incredible linguistic gymnastics, but was it really necessary to burden our minds with this nonsense ? There was a craze for classification and subdivision, which was regarded as a good thing in itself. My own three children have had none of this, but they are just as fond of reading ; they regard a house without books as a poor place ; and they all write acceptable English in spite of having read History, Engineering, and Medicine. I liked Latin from the very beginning, for which I have to thank a brilliant teacher the Headmaster himself, and his choice of a Latin Grammar—the *Elementa Latina* by W. H. Morris, whose work had reached the 26th impression before I was born. We at once became aware of the connexion between English and Latin words—*victoria*, *nauta*, *vita*, *porta*, *servus*, *equus*, *amicus*, *vicus*, *liber*, *vir*, *faber*, each of the five declensions being rich in these related words. Some years ago I saw a text book called *Latin for Today*, and I thought it was utterly wishy-washy lacking the essentially robust quality of the Latin on which I had been reared. Attempts to jazz up the dignified old Roman tongue must always end in failure. There was something very satisfactory for beginners in translating Latin into,—' Galba gives an arrow '—obviously a nice chap. ' Battles give victory ; victory gives life ' ; and on to the slightly more advanced, ' The citizens were fearing lest Rome might be surrounded by the Gauls ' ; and the same Gauls were worried,—' lest the hostages might have been killed by

Caesar '. When after a year we started on Caesar's *De Bello Gallico*, Book V, I thought at once that here was the Latin style I'd like to emulate. I have never lost my enthusiasm for Caesar—a very great man, and a performer of mighty deeds—it was always a delight to arrive at his ' *Eo cum venisset*(*s*) or his Ablative Absolutes, for then you could expect positive action. ' *Eo cum venisset, animum advertit and alteram fluminis ripam magnas esse copias hostium instructas* '. ' Having got there he noticed large forces of the enemy drawn up on the other side ',—not an easy man to hoodwink—or ' *Eo cum venisset, civitatibus milites imperat certumque in locum convenire iubet* '. ' Having got there, he demands troops from the states and orders them to gather at a certain spot '. Caesar was a most fascinating Roman, and the greatest war correspondent of all time. When we had read large chunks of Caesar,—we felt we knew him as a man. But life was earnest, and our care-free gambols amid the pages of *Elementa Latina* and *De Bello Gallico* were rudely interrupted by initiation into the styles of Livy and Cicero, backed up by North and Hillard *Latin Prose Composition for the Middle Forms of Schools* ! My edition from Foyles was dated 1895. The dear old *Elementa Latina* had to resign pride of place to Kennedy's *Latin Grammar*, re-inforced by a veritable cloud of little booklets which were used for prose unseens. Some of the fun went out of our Latin studies then. I much preferred Livy to Cicero, and still remember vividly his description of the Roman senators in their ivory chairs committing suicide rather than fall to the tender mercies of the barbarians. But best of all was Virgil, whose appeal was immediate and intoxicating. When Dr. Rees was reciting Virgil's description of the capture of Troy, with Aeneas carrying his aged father Anchises and the household gods away from the devasted city, through the flames, we were moved almost to tears. He also told us how it happened that Aeneas was the son of Venus as a consequence of some care-free frolics on Mount Ida.

I made the occasional sixpence or shilling, by tutoring some of those boys and girls who had not prepared their homework for the day, the individual fee being a halfpenny or a penny. It did not last, because one or two of the ' wide ' boys would buy my version, and then undersell my original work to the *poloi*—that's what life is more often than not !

Dr. Rees was a genius at teaching, not only Latin, but English Literature also. He taught from great strength as he had been a student for many years and the Headship of the Grammar School was his first post. He had been elected to a Chair, I think at

Aberystwyth, but as he was a Unitarian, the strongly entrenched Methodist vested interest objected. What a loss to them, and a gain to us ! He had studied in depth Sanskrit, Greek, Latin, German, and French. He was born at Llandysul on a small holding, and went after his local schooling to the Unitarian College, Carmarthen, then to the University College of Wales at Aberystwyth. From there to Oxford and London where he obtained his M.A., being placed top of all the candidates in Great Britain. Then he passed several years at the University in Leipsig where he was awarded his doctorate. German scholars maintained that his German was perfect. The declaration of war in 1914 was a terrible shock to him. From Leipsig this paragon of a wandering scholar went via Italy, to the Sorbonne in Paris, where he re-furbished his old skill in French. He must have been over thirty when he came to take charge of the small Free Grammar School in Cardigan. In 1917 there were 270 pupils on the roll—which was a record ! This great Headmaster in addition to teaching us some of the subjects on the time-table taught us manners—and this chiefly by his own example and code of behaviour. You raised your cap to all females, whom you passed on the pavement by taking the side next the street ; you opened doors for girls inside school—you called all teachers Sir or Miss ; there were no married ladies on the staff. If you had no head-gear you bowed, a slight inclination of the head. He himself tilted his hat forwards by the rear brim when he acknowledged our salutes. We were to begin with, a pretty bucolic lot, much in need I should say of some formal training in those courtesies, which made social life pleasant. I recall how movingly he recited to us, when we were doing Julius Caesar, Antony's eulogy of Brutus,—

> ' This was the noblest Roman of them all :
> All the conspirators, save only he,
> Did that they did in envy of great Caesar ;
> He only, in a general honest thought,
> And common good to all, made one of them.
> His life was gentle ; and the elements
> So mixt in him, that Nature might stand up
> And say to all the world, ' This was a man '.

He expatiated on the maxim ' manners makyth man ', and on the importance, nay the imperative necessity of having a personal code of conduct. Of him, too, generations of pupils have said,—' This was a man '. He was a great stylist, and was a handsome man with a well-kept beard, which legend held, was grown to conceal his student duelling scars. He dressed well—a high starched collar and double-breasted suits, which his son Brigadier Vivian Rees informed me, were made by Harrods for him. And in Summer it was a joy to see him leaving the Boat Club impeccably dressed in white flannels, handling his skiff with that deceptive ease which was perfection. In fact everything he did was stylishly done ; there was no room for the sloppy or the slip-shod in his creed. He believed in thoroughness—and so in Latin he saw to it that we had more than covered the syllabus before an examination. He was particularly fond of any word or construction that was irregular, and would write a tag or two on the black-board to assist our memory, such as,—

' *Tolle me, mu, mi, mis,*
Si declenare domus vis '.

So infectious was his own enthusiasm, that he could gather us into his confidence as accomplices. The gerund and the gerundive, do not at first sight appear promising fodder for an afternoon lesson, but so deftly did he deploy his fascinating skill that the whole form had grasped their use and nuances by the time the bell went. As a result of his teaching most of us gained passes with Distinction or Credit, except one girl who was awarded a Pass ! He insisted she should sit the exam again the next time round, which she did and gained a Credit, thus satisfying honour on both sides.

But if we concede that as a teacher of Latin he was at the top, in English literature he was a veritable Pied Piper. Many a time and oft, when the bell rang to announce the change over, while he was holding forth, a sigh of regret would be involuntarily heaved by the whole form. He even made Carlyle palatable ! He would not allow us to confine our attention only to texts set for examination. He ranged far and wide, and we a happy throng went along joyfully with him. He read us selections of Browning at a time when that author was reserved for University reading—and how utterly magical it was, when he described Fiesole, Florence, the Guelphs and Ghibellines, Giotto's circle, Dante, Michael Angelo, the leaning Tower of Pisa, and the ancient universities of Bologna and Padua. The School was not equipped with a stage for Dramatics, but as he said, this was no obstacle—so we acted all our plays—miming the opening of doors, and ignoring the absence of costume. What a brilliant Shylock he was, with unutterable pathos in his voice when he slowly answered Portia's final question,—

' Art thou contented, Jew ? What dost thou say ? '

' *I am content* '.

Then he would explain that Shakespear had probably never met a Jew, for the Jews had been expelled by Edward I in 1290, and were not allowed to return till after Cromwell's Whitehall Conference of 1677. He taught us to loathe persecution wherever it was found, and never to join a mob shouting ' Crucify Him ', ' Stone Him ', ' Kill Him '. ' You have been endowed with brains—use them to make your own decisions '. He did not encourage us to read what critics wrote about the authors we had to study, he told us to read the original works and make our own judgements in that way, we too might become original. I remember his teaching of Keats, and in particular the *Ode to Autumn*. Coming to the end, he suddenly asked me for a phrase of only a few words which would describe the Ode, so taken by surprise I blurted out ' withering beauty '. My class-mates laughed, but he said it was not a bad unprepared reply. I was teased in break next day about my answer, but as I was quite tough, and not at all averse to a rough house, this did not last long. Yet I was maturing but slowly. In one of the examinations—it might have been the Junior, the candidate was invited to quote the important parts of Gray's *Elegy* and *The Ancient Mariner*. I liked both, and could recite both off by heart, for I never went anywhere without a cheap paper copy of each—Blackie's price 2d, I think, and so had read them so often that I was word perfect. In my arrogant innocence, I informed the Examiner that in my opinion, both pieces were worthy to be quoted *in toto*, and so I wrote about half of each on my script. Alas ! I had a long way still to travel, but Dr. Rees had given me an understanding of vital basic principles, or as he would have said, ' put us on the road '.

His death was typical of this cultured man. When he retired, he went away from the town and settled in Hastings. Then one day he wanted to verify certain things in Carthage, so in his forthright way he took a train to Italy whence he would cross to Tunis. He was not well before he started off from England, but he grew steadily worse and passed away in the train near Turin. A year before he died he wrote from Hastings to me at Oxford.

' My dear Williams,

It was a great pleasure to hear from you again and to find that you are still pegging away at it. Many people in your position would long since have rested on their oars and settled down to a hum-drum existence—and probably cursed fate for not giving them a better chance in life. You, I am glad to find, are not one of those ; you still see ' fresh worlds to conquer ' ; and, depend upon it, by stepping on from one thing to another, you are making the best of life and getting the best out of it. Like myself you arrived at Oxford rather late in life : that could not be helped ; but the great thing is that you got there and, with your experience of men and things, you are in a position to take in the best of what Oxford has to offer—which is probably the best of what the world has to offer. The memory of it all will be for you a joy for ever which nothing and no one can take away from you —I congratulate you very heartily on your successes : it is fortunate that you are able to take your examinations in your stride, and it is well to go on qualifying in various directions : all these things tell, and they may come in handy some day : in any case they add to your mental stock-in-trade and enable you, as I used to tell you in the old days, to hold your head up with the consciousness that there was something in it !—I was sorry to read what you say about the old school : I had already heard rumours of developments impossible in the past : but there is still scope for good work there and excellent material to work upon—so let us hope everybody will rise to the height of the opportunity. We are both of us well and my wife joins me in sending our very best wishes.

Yours sincerely,

D. Rees '.

Young graduates of today will be amazed how low teachers' salaries were in those days. In 1917 Dr. Rees needed a qualified person, to teach French. There were twenty-eight applicants, and a woman with 1st Class Honours was appointed. The Salary scales advertised were £130—£230 for men and £120—£200 for women. These figures illustrate the extent of the inflation of the last fifty years. When I was an undergraduate you could take a girl out for a lavish evening, if you had two half-crowns in your pocket. Life has certainly become more complicated, but not better, we abandon simplicity at our peril.

There was one incident at school for which all of us who were responsible still feel sorry. A pretty Girton girl with plaits of gorgeous golden hair wreathing her head, was appointed to teach us elementary German. We boys were most impressed and believed outselves to be in love with her. Aren't schoolboys always falling in love with the older and more sophisticated girl ? One day she appeared sad and off colour, and I remember in answer to her, ' *Was ist das*? ' she pointing to a book, I replied, ' *Das ist ein buch* ', but giving the *buch* the exaggerated Welsh pronunciation of *bwch* which means a billy-goat. My mates dutifully laughed, and she burst into tears. We did not know what to do—the girls called us all kinds of names and surrounded the teacher—wiped her dry, and very gamely she continued the lesson, after sportingly saying she wasn't herself that day. Later we discovered that she had heard that very morning of the death in action of her fiancé. We now felt less than the dust ; no immolation would be too great for us, so when she came to us for the next lesson we all stood up and made our apologies. There never was any more nagging after that. Until her death last year I used to have the most pleasant chats with her. I still think she was a real sweetie.

The chemistry master was one of the most successful teachers, and his handling of apparatus superbly skilful. We had to write up our experiments in the red notebooks, underlining in red all titles and sub-headings. When he was angry he developed a twitch. Boys did silly things in the lab—one, now a retired headmaster, is still minus one eye after experimenting on his own with explosive substances. Another boy thought it funny to disconnect a rubber tube through which chlorine was passing. We all coughed frantically and were driven outside until the lab was decontaminated.

In 1917 the news came that Lieutenant Madoc Jones, known as Silent Jones, had been killed in France. He was a fine figure of a man, and he had taught us French. His family endowed a fund to give a certain number of ' Character Prizes ' to boys and girls of the school each year. The prizewinners were selected by a joint vote of Staff and Pupils. I was one of them, and I chose a beautiful leather bound volume of Wordsworth's poetry. Would I have been one of them if Staff alone, or School alone had been sole arbiters ? I shall never know, but I was very pleased with my prize which I still have. But another much earlier prize in History entitled *The Thirsty Sword*, I have mislaid, but I thought then that it was an excellent book written in an attractive style. Our History Master could get us through exams, but he was no disciplinarian. He could not take a joke, so he was ragged. Two boys who regularly baited him sat close together in a double desk. When he asked something like, ' Why did Wolsey fall ? ' the boy next to the master would reply,—' Because he could not stand, Sir ', knowing that a cuff on the ear would be aimed at him. He would smartly duck while his neighbour would allow himself to be hit, thereupon raising a dreadful howl—' Sir, Sir, why do you hit me ? ' Often the ensuing pandemonium would develop into a chase by the tortured master after the boy, who would rush down the long corridor to the boys' cloakroom, and there could dodge capture indefinitely. Then the Headmaster or an Assistant would emerge from another room, and suggest that if the games were over, perhaps a little less noise would be forthcoming from our form-room, etc., etc., the usual pedagogic humour. He succeeded Miss James, M.A., Lond., a degree which was then considered by us to be the pinnacle of academic achievement. She was no disciplinarian either. She was a little woman, always dressed in a skirt, blouse and jacket. Deep in her scanty bosom somewhere was a gold watch which was attached to a very long fine gold chain. We always asked her the time, so that we could be regaled by the sight of the watch being hauled from the mysterious depths where it reposed, just like the woman of Samaria hauling up her bucket of cool water from the depths of Jacob's well in the time of Christ. When she took charge of the Detention Class in the Central Hall on Wednesday afternoon—she would soon fall fast asleep in her armchair. We would then tie a thin rope to the chair's legs, and ever so gently draw the chair and Miss James across the polished floor to an adjoining room. Then most of us would quietly leave for home. She left teaching to go to a nunnery, where it is hoped there were no discipline problems, only naughty monks to pull her leg.

There was always homework—which if neglected lost you Wednesday half-holiday, when there was no school. This mid-week half-holiday was a most refreshing institution. In summer it meant the sea-side—or fishing for mackerel, or a long cycle ride. Sometimes several boys would transport the girls along with them, the girls sitting on the handlebars of the bike, and leaning back comfortably,—we hoped confidently, on the manly chest. It must be remembered these were the days of stone-metalled roads—no macadam—and after rain they were very slippery. Ruts were formed by the iron-tyred wheels of the carts, gambos, brakes and waggons. We never travelled without a good repair outfit and a pump, for sharp stones often penetrated the soft outer cover causing the air to escape from the tube. At night one had a carbide lamp, which was very effective.

Games were not compulsory in my day, but there was one match we did not willingly miss,—Girls versus Boys, at hockey. We played rugger and hockey only casually and occasionally. We boys were penalised for raising our sticks above the shoulder, and for nearly every other transgression in the book. Needless to add the girls always won. These were the pre-bra days so the lumpy girls usually press-ganged a big scarf secured with safety-pins to do what was needed. Mrs. Mary Caresse Crosby who died in Rome in January 1970 is credited with the invention of the ' bra ', although she always denied it. It is likely that many women (and men ?) had ideas about it. Our girls certainly knew how to improvise one. There was one outstanding player, and she went on to play for the University and for Wales. It was she who was knocked out by a shinty-style stroke from an over-enthusiastic boy,—me !

Of the twenty-nine pupils in my form at school, over twenty went to universities, which was a highly creditable result from a small country school. As I have said before, we had to buy our books, and W. & G. Foyle of Charing Cross Road, could supply all our needs, the prices ranging from 3d. to 1/6d. Many years later William Foyle was a Governor of a school of which I was Headmaster. He lived at Beeleigh Abbey, near Maldon, Essex,—an enchanting residence which he averred was haunted. He was a pixilated Puck-like man with beautiful silver hair with a perfect sense of hospitality. There was nothing mean about him, for in his early days he had known poverty. He had converted the monks' dormitory of the Abbey into a library to house an impressive collection of books, which today, only millionaires could covet successfully. He had first editions by the dozen, including the first, second and third folios of Shakespeare—and French classics bound in rich coloured leather. One was an exquisite fake which he used for a practical joke. It looked exactly like a first folio volume, and on handing it to you he'd say, ' Look at that—how much do you think it's worth ? ' You opened it reverently and saw enshrined inside the text a bottle of the best cognac with 4 glasses—which he would proceed to fill amid jolly laughter all round. A sweet old gentleman. His daughter Christina was our Guest of Honour one Speech day, and she was splendid, a real chip of the old block. The secret of the charm of the Foyles was that they had no foolish ' side ', they were real people, and behaved as such. They have deserved the success which has attended their activities among books.

The years I spent at the Grammar School saw the rise and fall of several amateur magazines. I became the self-appointed editor of the *Rambler* and the *Spectator*—but neither survived for more than a few numbers. In my need I was promised a sparkling contribution by Norah, an exuberant pretty girl in our form, in return for a verse in praise of her beauty. I set to and produced a bilingual version which pleased her mightily but, fickle girl, she never fulfilled her side of the bargain. The verses were sung to the tune of *The Ash Grove.*

In the village of Llechryd on the banks of the Teify
There lives a fair maiden in happiness there.
To describe this bright mortal, indeed she's so lovely,
Is hard, for such blossoms are awfully rare.
Her voice is pure sweetness, her eyes deep and tender
Her face is as bright as the break of the dawn.
She carries herself with as refined a manner,
Her form is so graceful, her heart is so warm.

As a matter of fact she had a very fine singing voice, but her deep tender eyes were those of an uninhibited flirt. The Welsh version gets nearer to some sort of poetic utterance.

Ym mhentref bach Llechryd ar lannau y Teifi
Mae geneth lon hyfryd yn byw yno'n awr,
Ei enw yw Nora, mae'n un or prydfertha'
Ei gwyneb sy'n dyner fel awel y wawr.
Tynerwch a chariad fe gewch yn ei llygad
Ei llais fel rhyw eos yn canu'n y llwyn
Mae serch lond ei chalon, a lifa fel afon,
Anaml cael cystal cymeriad mor fwyn.

It was Andrew, a versatile genius if ever there was one, who produced a paper which was a popular success for many years. It contained news of the war, local scandals, genuine news items such as the list of the winners at the various concerts and *eisteddfodau*, ballads, advertisements, indignant letters to the Editor—written mostly by himself, and of course contributions from his numerous friends. It caught the local imagination, and the paper was eagerly circulated from one hand to another. Andrew wrote a ballad, which we, who knew the persons mentioned in it found very funny. He called it,—

Zeppelins over Cardigan by Andrew Havard Williams.

The air was heavy, the night was dark
For no moon was shining.
Dark clouds obscured the heavens above
Indeed the scene was trying.

But all of a sudden there came a roar,—
The sound of bombs a-dropping.
And far above the Cardigan folk
The Zeppelins were flying.

The first bomb was dropped on Cardigan Bridge,
And down went many a girder.
Locket bâch was seeing all this
And shouted ' Murder ! Murder !

The next was dropped on S. T. Jones
The eminent ironmonger.
He ran across to Manchester House
And sprawled all oe'r the counter.

Mrs. Davies soon came up
And many other faces
Go away ! Go away ! cried S. T. Jones
I'm in a thousand pieces.

The next was dropped on the Market Hall,
And another on Bowen Brothers,
Out came Clougher in great wrath,
And with him Rees the Grocers.

And soon the Square was packed and crushed
To witness the proceedings
A British aeroplane flew past
'T'was welcomed with joyful cheerings.

Out came T.M. as white as chalk,
And with him Howell Morgan
He whispered softly to Twm Turn
Let's pray, and play the organ.

And then a crashing sound was heard,
And to its doom descended,
The wretched Huns with their Zepp
And now the fun was ended.

And everything did quiet down
For now the Zepp had gone
So dear boys and also girls
I bid you all so-long.

Another war poem which won applause was this by Griffith J. James.

The Kaiser has with all his might
Been long preparing for this fight,
Yet even now he won't confess
That he has caused so much distress.
A ' baby-killer ' he is named
For causing murders he is fam'd
Ere long some ' Tommy Atkins ' will
Fix bayonet and push through Bill.

A thing not understood by the youth of today was the organisation of our own fun and games. We would meet in a double piggery long abandoned by those for whom it was destined, and arrange various competitions and programmes calculated to entertain. One such came to a sudden end. The prize was for the best single act by a boy or a girl. We assembled in our piggery—with candles in jam-jars to light up the scene. For some reason not immediately comprehended David John Lloyd brought in some hay, and a soap box. The announcer—Andrew— in an early Sachs manner wittily introduced Davi John, who was going to demonstrate '*Bathing at Brighton*' and in he came completely nude, stood on his box, and dived into the hay—amid loud applause. Hardly had the excitement subsided, when the piercing voice of Phoebe his mother was heard immediately outside shouting ' Davi John where art thou ? ' ' I'm in here Mother, I can't come out yet—I shall be too cold without my clothes '. ' No, you won't my boy, not when I've finished smacking your bottom '. David John like our first father Adam was hiding because he was naked. Phoebe and the Lord both called out, ' Where art thou ? ', and both meted out punishment, but Phoebe's was infinitely less severe than that imposed by the Lord God of the Old Testament.

Another event was the trial run of the Williams and Williams aeroplane. We decided to have a Mechanical Exhibition where any original invention could be entered. Andrew and I chose to build an aeroplane which would be able to proceed under its own power on the road. The prize was 4 bottles of pop. We appointed the local blacksmith Tommy Thomas as consultant engineer. This fine old character would drink half a gallon of beer without taking the tankard from his mouth if you paid for it. We proceeded to work ; all our pocket money going to pay for bolts, nuts, and other materials. The wings which together spanned 12 feet were made from canvas stretched on a primitive geodetic framework with paper pasted on to it. The fuselage was a long spruce pole 14 feet long on which were located in line astern two Tate and Lyle 1 cwt. loaf-sugar boxes bolted together. These comprised the cockpits for pilot and observer. The pilot operated the stick which through a system of wires controlled a small perambulator wheel in a shortened bicycle fork at the tail, just below the rudder. It was direct steering—very violent in its effect, as, given space the whole contraption could turn in an exceedingly tight circle. A big 2 blade propeller in front was turned by the same bicycle chains which transferred man-power to the pair of bicycle landing wheels on which the whole machine rested. We made a crank for these chains, and the person in the front cockpit (sugar box no. 1) had all his work cut out to get up a speed of about one mile an hour. However, the great day came, and one summer evening with quite a crowd assembled, we proceeded downhill towards Cardigan. I steered it along the middle of the road. Rounding the first bend we saw to our horror Mr. Williams the solicitor and his family coming towards us in a governess trap. The sight of this strange monster terrified the pony, who stood up on his hind legs—pivoted round smartly and deposited his passengers in the ditch. We equally promptly put on opposite rudder and crashed into the hedge—then over a convenient gate and back home by a devious route. Dear old Mr. Williams when he had recovered thought it was a good joke, and gave Andrew and me half a crown each when he next met us—to repair the aeroplane, he said, for its next flight. This next flight was a final disaster, for we took it to a steep hill and allowed a pretty girl to come as a passenger. She, not the girl, responded very sluggishly to the controls, and as speed increased she began to ' hunt ' and finally crashed into a wall, buckling both landing wheels and the propeller. We surveyed the damage ruefully, decided to call it a day, for although we knew the thing could have flown one day—we had no more money left, either to undertake repairs to this model or pay for the design of an improved Mark II.

Many of the pupils came from up to fifteen miles away, and in the absence of public transport, they lodged in one of the registered lodgings, where they had to be in by seven at night. Occasionally the Headmaster would call round to make a spot check. There was no school meals service, so we all brought our lunches with us and went into the local coffee tavern for a cup of tea. I had an Aunt, a widow, who ran a livery stables in the town, and sometimes I'd have a good square meal there—in return for which I prepared some bills for her. She allowed credit for one year ! Her horses were beautiful, and she had an old ship's painter named Davy Jones to paint and varnish the brakes, gigs, broughams, and waggonettes, which were housed in a huge hangar-like shed. She also had a brisk haulage trade. Her two sons were not very enterprising, and when the T model Ford came out, I tried to persuade her to become mechanised, but in vain, so after her death, the successful business she had built up just lapsed by default. But Davy Jones, what a man—and what stories of the sea. His cottage behind the coach hangar was only two rooms, but he had a lovely fire at all times. Seated in his windsor chair, hands clasped across his generous paunch, thumbs rhythmically twiddling, he'd unfold a tale—and we boys listened enthralled. One of his best stories was about rounding the Horn—so cold it was that men's feet swelled to the size of pumpkins, and then beating up the coast of South America, they'd call at various ports doing quite a bit of coastal trading. Once when they were ashore they were shown by the natives how to catch monkeys. A cocoanut was opened, the aperture being large enough for a monkey to insert his paw, and this was tethered by a knotted lanyard through the soft eye, and pegged to the ground. A dollop of demarara was placed inside, and you retired to watch events. Curiosity overcoming discretion the monkeys would shin down from the trees to examine the nuts—then tentatively taste the brown sugar—and alas ! overcome by greed would shove their hand inside, and clutch as much sugar as was possible. They were trapped for the clenched paw full of sugar was too big to be withdrawn. You rushed out, held the animal by the scruff of his neck, then grimacing fearsomely, you bit his paw hard. The old salt swore that the monkey would never dare bite you after that. Before he died he had asked for the boys who had listened to his tales over the years, to be the bearers at his funeral. At the graveside it was pouring with rain, and the lines which we had to lower him into his grave were so slippery that, ' steady as he goes ', could not be maintained, so Davy Jones came to rest leaning against the West in a comfortable reclining position gazing towards the East. How he, the central character, would have enjoyed the joke. The committal service proceeded with him in this position which permitted him to have a watching brief.

I kept my bike in the nearest village about a mile and a half away, for in winter particularly, access to our home was very difficult. I have seen carts getting stuck having sunk up to their axles, so with a huge leather satchel on my back I walked through woods, along the sides of fields crossing the river three or four times, and learning something new about Nature every day. In spite of this long journey, I was absent for an average of only two half days per year, and late about twelve times. On arriving home there were always jobs to do—clean pig sties, tie the cattle in the cowshed, and in winter cut enough hay for a day or two—feed warm milk with crusts of stale bread in it to calves. Then a hot meal of delicious *cawl* and bread and butter. Homework followed, and if that went well I'd read. I was an indiscriminate reader ; I'd read anything rather than not read at all. I read a great deal of rubbish, and books that were too ' old ', or too ' young ' for me such as *John Halifax Gentleman*, (over 400 pages), *Jessica's First Prayer*, *Tamil the Elephant.* My regular diet of reading was dictated by the availability of books to my taste—tales of adventure on land and on sea. My eldest sister received a prize at a Christmas party,—*Hurricane Hurry*,—by William H. G. Kingston, published in 1873, nearly 600 pages in length. I loved it. Like all the Victorian books a high moral tone was set, and prayer was resorted to as a matter of routine. When the tempest roared, words were addressed, ' to Him who alone can quell the tempest '. But there was action in abundance with ample technical jargon, ' the crew had come aft to take in the mainsail and gaff topsail. I next had the fore top-gallant-sail and foresail off her. Up with the helm ! In with the main-staysail ! Square away the fore-yard. Hold on for your lives ! ' Kingston wrote several other books, and in common with other Victorian authors, he made no concession by way of a simplified vocabulary for children. The age of ' pappy ' children's books had not yet come. If I had time I'd look up hard words in a dictionary, but more often than not I guessed their meaning from the context. These writers considered our feelings to be a legitimate target on which to work. In *The Early Life of Old Jack* we are quickly introduced to tragedy, ' Why won't Father speak to me ? ' I asked, dreading the answer. ' He'll never speak again ! Your father's dead, lad ', answered the man, in a tone of commiseration '. If you liked this volume you could follow the fortunes of our hero in *Old Jack as a Man-of-War's Man.* Another of Kingston's books was a favourite with me. *The Three Midshipmen,* Jack, Dick, and Paddy. It started well, ' Ours was a capital school, though it was not a public one . . .', so old Etonians did not have the privilege of winning all the naval engagements, as well as Waterloo. These three midshipmen provided another three volumes for Kingston,—*The Three Lieutenants*, the

Three Commanders, and *The Three Admirals*. I was fond of poaching, and in *Peter the Whaler* Kingston contrives to have Peter, who was a good shot, sentenced by Lord Fetherston the magistrate, to a life at sea. I burned with indignation at the injustice of it. Still, we have not advanced very far, for quite recently in Scotland, a London holiday-maker was cast into prison for helping a native take a salmon out of the water. I wrote an indignant letter to John Gordon of the Daily Express about it, and he managed to get a Queen's pardon for him. G. H. Henty was another author who fed my insatiable appetite for adventure with substantial contributions like,—' *In Times of Peril* ; *One of the 28th* ; *With Clive in India* ; *Under Wellington's Command* ; *The Lion of the North* ; *March on London* ; *Wulf the Saxon* ; and *True to the Old Flag*, a tale of the American War of Independence. A book for which I had a great regard was *The Heroes*, by Charles Kingsley, which Dr. Rees read with us at odd times in Latin lessons. Those ancient Greeks were men of deep cunning, but their strategems were understood and admired by us, as for instance, when Theseus secured his safe return from the labyrinth by following a clue of thread ; it made good sense. The only other works by Kingsley read by me in those days were *Westward Ho* ! *Hereward the Wake* and *The Water Babies*. Much more attractive were the stories by R. M. Ballantyne,—*Martin Rattler* ; *The Coral Island* ; *The Gorilla Hunters* ; *The Young Fur Traders* ; and *The Dog Crusoe*, whose father and mother were magnificent Newfoundlanders. Crusoe's career was nearly cut short when an Indian squaw was about to put him in the pot before Varley intervened. I must not omit Captain Marryat, R.N., whose books were available for 6d., as well as in the de luxe 3/6d. editions for prizes. In the cheap editions there were advertisements —including the famous one of Pears' Soap. ' Pure, Fragrant, and Durable ' (a good point for soap was expensive, in fact, good soap has never been cheap) ; ' The Best for The Skin ', and if you had doubts about this in the absence of last century's Katie Boyle, the advert informed you that it was ' Recommended by Professor Sir Erasmus Wilson, President of the Royal College of Surgeons '. Of Marryat's books I liked best *Mr. Midshipman Easy*, *The Settlers in Canada*, *Peter Simple*, *Children of the New Forest*, *The Little Savage*, or *Adventures on a Desert Island*, *The Poacher*, and *Masterman Ready*. Marryat's plots were sketchy to a degree, but he drew splendid characters and could etch dramatic situations. Regardless of rank, his characters expressed themselves in impeccable English. In the *Poacher*, when Rushbrook and Jane had returned to their cottage, and had closed the door, Jane threw herself into her husband's arms, 'You are saved, at least', she cried ; 'thank Heaven for that ! You are spared. Alas ! we do not know how much we love till danger comes upon us'. Rushbrook was much affected ; he loved his wife, and had good reason to love her. Jane was a beautiful woman, not yet thirty ; tall in her person, her head was finely formed, yet apparently small for her height ; her features were full of expression and sweetness. Had she been born to a high station she would have been considered one of the great belles'. One winter's night with the family gathered around I was reading *Masterman Ready*, and came to where Ready was fatally wounded while fetching water for those inside the stockade, 'Are you hurt, Ready ?' said William. 'Yes, dear boy, yes ; hurt to death I fear, his spear went through my breast. Water, quick, water'.

When the old man's head fell backward, and he was no more, the opportunity to improve the tragic occasion was not missed by Mr. Seagrave who mournfully announced, 'It is all over, and he has, I have no doubt, gone to receive the reward of a good and just man. Happy are those who die in the Lord'. I was so overcome by emotion that I quietly left the room, and walked about outside in the cold air till there was no likelihood of my disgracing myself in public, by an undue show of feeling. Recently I re-read that part, and remained completely unmoved. What else did I read ? There were the *Conquest of Peru*, 2 vols, *The Conquest of Mexico*, 2 vols, *Ferdinand and Isabella*, 2 vols.,—and *Philip II*, 2 vols. Where I borrowed them from I am not sure, but it might have been the Mechanics Institute, which I frequented daily in term time. Here were the Encyclopaedias, and a series of red-coloured volumes of extracts from the World's best literature. Here too I read *Rienzi*, *The Last Days of Pompeii*, *The Last of the Barons*, and Hawthorn's *Scarlet Letter*, *The House of the Seven Gables*, *Twice Told Tales*, and a little known book by James Grant, entitled *The Romance of War*. Of Cooper's works I read only *The Last of the Mohicans*, *Deerslayer*, and *Pathfinder*. For some reason I cannot fathom, both boys and girls were expected to read William Harrison Ainsworth's *Tower of London*, *Guy Fawkes*, and *Old Saint Paul's*. At school we had to read Lamb's *Essays*, and they were beautifully written, but I could not abide Ruskin—I thought then and still think that he is an overrated author. Some authors acquired reputations at bargain prices ! Our M.P.'s mother often lent me books, two of the best being *Tom Sawyer* and *Hucklebury Finn*.

I read Scott but felt his novels were too wordy, and too long-drawn-out. I liked best but without enthusiasm *Ivanhoe*, *Kenilworth*, *Rob Roy*, *The Abbot*, *Quentin Durward*, and *Redgauntlet.* I read some Dickens, but the only work of his I liked was *The Tale of Two Cities.* Thackeray I could not get on with at all, but Trollope I thought was splendid. My biggest regret now is, that no one put me in touch with Jane Austen. I had enjoyed books by another woman-writer George Eliot,—*Adam Bede*, *Romola*, *The Mill on the Floss*, and also *Jane Eyre* and *Wuthering Heights* of the Brontês, but somehow I was not introduced to Miss Austen the greatest woman writer of all, till I was at the University. What a talented woman, what a perfectionist ! Her best, I think, is *Pride and Prejudice*, which the publisher Cadell rejected by return of post. Publication is more often than not a matter of luck, a joint gamble for author and publisher.

We had a successful local writer who wrote under the pseudonym Allen Raine. She was Mrs. Anne Adalisa Puddicombe (1836—1908) —the eldest child of Benjamin Evans, solicitor of Newcastle-Emlyn. Her mother was the daughter of Thomas Morgan the surgeon. She was educated at Carmarthen, Cheltenham and Wimbledon ; became an accomplished musician, and knew French, Italian and colloquial Welsh. In 1872 she married Beynon Puddicombe of Smith Payne's Bank, London, and they set up a home near Croydon, but here Allen Raine suffered continuous ill-health. In 1900 her husband became mentally ill, and they came to Tresaith to live in their holiday cottage where in 1906 he died, to be followed by his wife in June 1908. Her first book *Myfanwy* was rejected by six publishers. She changed its title to *A Welsh Singer* by Allen Raine, and it was published by Hutchinsons in 1897 and 197,000 copies were sold. As a novelist, she did not hesitate to stretch co-incidence to its limits ; for instance, in *A Welsh Singer*, when the bull gores John Powys, Sir Glynne who was witnessing the attack, happens to have handy, a red silk handkershief to distract the beast's attention. A stiff upper lip was preserved in all circumstances,—' And with the British dislike of a scene, the two men parted with a warm clasp of the hand and nothing more '. The influence of Queen Victoria and the *pukka sahibs* was then at its height. The *Daily Mail* book reviewer wrote, ' Wales has waited long for her novelist ; but he seems to have come at last in the person of Mr. Allen Raine who in his perfectly beautiful story, *A Welsh Singer*, has at once proved himself a worthy interpreter of the romantic spirit of his country '. Had the reviewer known the author was a woman, he would not have written so kindly, for prejudice against women was then strong, and, as we all know, is still with us. Allen Raine is important as the forerunner of a long procession of women who have become authors in this century, and who on the whole have written better than men. Allen Raine's success continued with *Torn Sails* 1898 (165,000 copies), *By Berwen's Banks* 1899 (141,000) ; *Garthowen* 1900 (152,000) ; *A Welsh Witch* 1902 (149,000) ; *On the Wings of the Wind* 1903 (144,000) ; *Hearts of Wales* 1905 (110,000) ; and *Queen of the Rushes* 1906, with incidents based on the Revival of 1904-5. After her death Hutchinsons issued her novels in 1909 in the 6d. series, and *Neither Storehouse nor Barn* appeared in this. There were well thumbed copies of the sixpenny series being handed round, when we were children, and pride in our local celebrity, as much as interest in her novels made us read them. I believe that girls enjoyed the simple but romantic love stories more than we did ; we preferred stories like *Robinson Crusoe* and other tales of adventure.

I have referred to women authors who followed Allen Raine ; any selection random or otherwise would have to include the following,—Margery Sharp, Rumer Godden, Alison Uttley, Mary Stewart, Helen Ashton, Noel Streatfield, Norah Lofts, Margery Allingham, Dorothy Sayers, Nancy Mitford, Virginia Woolf, V. Sackville West, Margaret Irwin, Jean Rhys, Hilda Lewis, Rebecca West, Stella Gibbons, M. J. Farrell, Muriel Spark, Constance Holme, Margery Bowen, Angela Thirkell, Mary McCarthy, Rose Macaulay, Elizabeth Jenkins, Ann Bridge, Josephine Tey, Elizabeth Goodge, 'Miss Read', Edna O'Brien, Margaret Drabble, Helen Simpson, Phyllis Bottome, Phyllis Bentley. I apologise if I have omitted the name of some splendid woman writer, but this list will suffice to convince male sceptics, that the female is just as good a writer as the male.

Two other great authors who escaped me at School were George Bernard Shaw and Thomas Hardy. I read both in my first year at the University, and was most affected by the style and content of Shaw's Prefaces and Plays, but of Hardy,—I thought, here is a real writer who pulls no punches, and like an ancient Greek playwright, sees to it that the hero or heroine has no escape from the inexorable fate which the gods have decreed. Poor, sweet Tess—she hadn't a chance, and neither had Jude, nor any of his other chief characters, but they were splendidly thrilling books to read. Having finished with his novels I went on to consume as a savoury his *Dynasts*. If a selection had to be made of Hardy's works my choice would be *The Woodlanders*, *Under the Greenwood Tree*, *The Return of the Native*, *The Mayor of Casterbridge*, *Far from the Madding*

Crowd, *Jude the/Obscure*, and *Tess of the D'Urbervilles*. This I suggest would be a satisfying feast for the most exacting connoisseur.

Chaucer, Shakespear, Milton, Wordsworth and Dryden, are our greatest poets, but I like old Chaucer best of all. I met him by chance. I bid sixpence at a sale for a pile of books, a very mixed bag consisting of *Good Words*, which was edited by Norman Macleod, D.D., collections of sermons, commentaries on part of the Bible, and an edition of the *Canterbury Tales*, edited I think by the Rev. Richard Morris. The archaic language was vastly intriguing, so with the help of the glossary and the notes, I slowly made some headway. I began to decipher and to appreciate the text. After this haphazard beginning my admiration for Chaucer grew steadily. To-day, Chaucer is available to all who can read and appreciate poetry, for Professor Nevill Coghill has made a superb rendering of The Canterbury Tales into modern rhyming couplets. Listen now to how Coghill has modernised Chaucer's portrait of eighteen year old Alison,[1] a saucy wench and an accomplished flirt.

She was a fair young wife, her body as slender
As any weasel's, and as soft and tender ;
She used to wear a girdle of striped silk ;
Her apron was as white as morning milk
Over her loins, all gusseted and pleated.
White was her smock ; embroidery repeated
Its pattern on the collar, front and back,
Inside and out ; it was of silk and black.
The tapes and ribbons of her milky mutch
Were made to match her collar to a touch ;
She wore a broad silk fillet, rather high,
And certainly she had a lecherous eye.
And she had plucked her eyebrows into bows ;
Slenderly arched they were and black as sloes ;
And a more truly blissful sight to see
She was than blossom on a cherry-tree,
And softer than the wool upon a wether ;
And by her girdle hung a purse of leather
Tasseled with silk and silver droplets pearled ;
If you went seeking up and down the world,

---

[1]I am grateful to Professor Cogill for permission to use his new, and he thinks, better version of Alison.

The wisest man you met would have to wrench
His fancy to imagine such a wench ;
And her complexion had a brighter tint
Than a new florin from the royal mint.
As to her song, it was as loud and quick
As any swallow's chirping on a rick.
And she would skip and play some game or other
Like any kid or calf behind its mother.
Her mouth was sweet as mead or honey—say
A hoard of apples lying in the hay.
Skittish she was, and jolly as a colt,
Tall as a mast and upright as a bolt
Out of a bow. Her collaret revealed
A brooch as big as boss upon a shield.
High shoes she wore, and laced them to the top.
She was a daisy, O a lollypop
For any nobleman to take to bed
Or some good man of yeoman stock to wed.

Today, how Alison would have made fast cars slow up ; dim old eyes shine and turn, were she to come back and walk up King's Road in Chelsea, or along the tow-path in Eights-week at Oxford, or, best of all saunter in Term-time on the Promenade at Aberystwyth. A trendy girl, but an immortal.

And consider how modern this diction is ; how true to real life,—

Now, gentlemen, this Gallant Nicholas
Began to romp about and make a pass
At this young woman, happening on her one day,
Her husband being out, down Osney way.
Students are sly, and giving way to whim,
He made a grab and caught her by the quim
And said, ' O God, I love you ! Can't you see
If I don't have you it's the end of me ? '
Then held her haunches hard and gave a cry
' O love-me-all-at-once or I shall die ! '
She gave a spring, just like a skittish colt
Boxed in a frame for shoeing, and with a jolt
Managed in time to wrench her head away,
And said, ' Give over, Nicholas, I say !
No, I won't kiss you ! Stop it ! Let me go
Or I shall scream ! I'll let the neighbours know !
Where are your manners ? Take away your paws ! '

This is a perfect description of what a bold likerous lad is apt to hear from his Alison of today, be it in Oxford or any other place where be ' goings-on '. It's heard at harvest time, especially when all is safely gathered in.

Chaucer begins his Miller's Tale thus :

> 'Whilom ther was dwellynge at Oxenford
> A riche gnof, that geestes helld to bord '.

Each time I have heard Michael Flanders singing ' It was a "gunoo" (gnu) ' I have wished he had woven another lyric around the gnof, the ' gunoof ' a word which Nevill Coghill respectfully renders as ' old codger '. What a delight if the genius of Swan and Flanders had joined the ' gunoo and the gunoof ', in yet another of their sparkling musical comments !

We boys formed an unofficial reading club, to buy papers like the *Penny Popular*, *Gem* or *Magnet.* I have a faint recollection that the *Penny Popular* had three stories per issue, a school story about Tom Merry and Co., a Sexton Blake detective yarn, and the adventures of Jack, Sam, and Pete the latter being a huge negro of splendid physique and character. There were longer stories incorporating these heroes available in books costing 3d. Hence the club—we all bought different titles and then passed them round.

One powerful side effect of the strong maritime and naval flavour of the books I read, was to make me determined ultimately to follow the sea as a career. The father of one of my friends lent me his copy of the *Manual of Seamanship* published by the Stationery Office. This became a *vade mecum*, and in it I swotted every nautical term that I came across in my reading. The sails of square-rigged ships at last made sense. Starting with the flying jib I could sketch or name them, from stem to stern, from the flying jib to the spanker. Many of them had lovely names, lower fore-top-gallant sail, main-royal, main sky-sail, lower mizen top-sail. Likewise the hull and standing rigging, the bowsprit, gammoning, dolphin-striker, flying jib-boom, bobstays, lubber-holes, futtock, shrouds. I also memorised semaphore signs, Morse, and the international code. I worked with ropes making knots, splices, and bends. Most useful on a farm were a fisherman's bend a reef-knot, a sheepshank and a bow-line. Broken ropes were mended by short-splices, but if they were too worn for further stresses and strains, we would set to and make grommets out of them for use as indoor quoits.

During the war there was a tremendous amount of work to be done on the under-staffed farms. Able bodied men were in the forces, and women with the aid of the young and the old, did all they could to keep the farms going. One year the harvest had all to be cut by sickles—the rainstorms had flattened the wheat, barley and oats to the ground. Tedious back-breaking work and our food was tea sweetened with treacle, and black bread with lumps of potato in it. The German U boats nearly starved us. I also went to my Uncle William's farm where we slaved till dark cutting corn with a scythe fitted with what was called a chair *cadair* long fingers of seasoned ash shaped like the blade, on which standing corn when cut fell neatly, and with an unbroken rhythmic swing the corn was cut and laid neatly in a row ready to be bound into sheaves. If the weather was good, it was not bound into sheaves till it had dried out a little. Again the food we ate was poor. My Uncle's wife was no cook but a drassock who would make do with the least, rather than make a real effort to maintain standards. I used to walk home in the dark completely exhausted after 12 hours hard scything. And how different was the meal my mother had ready—tasty, delicious and in every other way adequate.

Rabbits became increasingly important as the war dragged on. We joined with neighbours, to have a blitz on the warrens with ferret and nets. An albino ferret was bought by us from a breeder, Tom Price, so we just called our ferret Tom. The first time I handled him I was too sudden in my movements, so he bit my first finger right through, and was hanging on grimly with his red pupils glowing, until father quickly gutted a rabbit and slobbed a piece of its liver across his nose—when he at once released his hold. He was always muzzled when working, not with a brass ring and pin, but with a muzzle made from the soft twine securing a bag of Spillers flour, with the knots hammered flat. He was then put in a small bag with straw in it. Sometimes I carried him inside the lining of an old jacket which he would explore all round, poking out his nose in a tear by my armpit and sneeze to made it clear he wished to be stroked. It's not only human beings who like to be made a fuss of ; all animals respond to it. Tom had a little silver bell tied round his neck, so that when we were ferreting at night, we would hear him when he came out of the labyrinth of rabbit holes, and thus secure him. I loved the excitement of a nocturnal ferreting expedition with my father. We had dozens of nets which we carried round our necks—not very comfortable when they were wet. They were made by us at odd moments, using a home-made shuttle of seasoned oak. They were dyed in a strong mixture of oak bark well seethed. The two pegs, and the two pieces one at either end of the net which slid along the guide cords when the rabbit hurled itself into it, were also made of seasoned oak. Rabbits on a moonlit night would be out of their warrens feeding, but we had a black spaniel called Pank, which had been taught not to bark only whimper gently—which rounded them up and chased them in. We would then net each hole. We had cut away brambles on a previous reconnaissance, so access to the various outlets was possible. When Tom was put in, one could hear the thumping of the panic-stricken rabbits fleeing away from this dreaded weazel-like creature. Sometimes two rabbits rushing pell-mell would be caught in the same net, but more often the second one escaped. That was why it was imperative that the captured rabbit be quickly extricated from the net, given a death-dealing karate blow behind the ears, and the net re-set. If the rabbit was very tangled up, there was the choice of killing it inside the net and set a fresh net, or sit with one's bottom in the hole to block the exit of the other rabbits. In its panic a rabbit would keep on butting the obstructing backside, when it could be caught by a carefully inserted hand. As the night proceeded the weight of rabbits steadily increased, and we would hang several up in the branches of a tree to be recovered later. When we reached home in the small hours of the morning we would have a cup of tea and something with it, then set-to gutting all the rabbits. Their hind legs were secured by a slit between the main tendon and the bone of one leg, the other leg being pulled through it. Then a pole was inserted between the legs, and several rows filled a strong wicker hamper which was labelled Bookless Bros., A good clean rabbit fetched 6d. The rabbit as a contribution to the food of the nation during the War can hardly be over-estimated. This timid creature with its gargantuan appetite for green fodder, had a character composed of greed, panics, fears, and defeatism. It could outrun the weazel, and outweighted it many times, but it allowed itself to be caught at the weazel's pleasure. The only aggressiveness shown was when bucks in the presence of females would stand upright, stamp on the ground and make futile passes at one another, of which none was calculated to wound.

When scared a rabbit appeared to be blind. After the binder had reduced the field of corn to a small oasis yet uncut, the rabbit would make a dart for the hedge, following its usual trail. I used to lie in the hedge on top of the rabbit's well-trodden path, and watch it bounding unseeingly towards me. It would leap over my prostrate body and then I could pick it out of the air, deal it a death-blow, and wait for the next. I have even known the glory of fielding a rabbit in each hand. This is in no way a boast, for if the eye is true, the hand swift, the odds are heavily against the rabbit escaping. Father and I also set snares at dusk in neighbouring fields belonging to other farmers. Beside each snare was placed a piece of white china—part of a plate or broken cup or saucer. This would enable us to spot the location when going the rounds late that night, and at dawn the following morning when the rabbits would be collected, and the snares taken up. One old poacher we knew had a curious belief. He would urinate on his hands and on the string of the snares, for he claimed this would attract the rabbits from far and wide. Sometimes we dispensed with nets taking only guns and ferret. I noticed how much more accurately the men shot after a good lunch washed down with plenty of home-brewed. I still associate with these activities the food we carried with us ; huge chunks of pig brawn, slabs of rice pudding which had been slowly cooked in a deep milk bowl and cooled on the stone floor of the dairy, and eating with each, long slices of home-baked brown bread. The standard warning to a small boy wiring into such weighty fare was for him to take care lest it fall on his foot. Willie's mother, Dianah, made glorious cake for Christmas which was still moist and lovely in February. It had home-brewed beer as one of its ingredients. Her face would be wreathed in smiles of appreciation as we boys consumed an unlimited number of slices of her delicious cake on our return from a whole day's ferreting.

As the main component of a pie, a rabbit was superb. Mixed with pieces of old streaky belly bacon, well cured, and onions, with home-made crust enveloping all, it was a most delectable dish. Boiled with a lump of bacon it made a delicious *cawl*. Cold, the pieces of rabbit were a convenient meal with pieces of bread and butter. My sister often fried a disjointed rabbit using butter, bacon fat, or dripping. The work of the night being over, I'd fall into bed already occupied by a younger brother, callously placing my cold back against his warm one, to cull some instant warmth. The morning would come all too soon, with its cowshed chores, and then away to school half-doped by lack of sleep and fatigue. In my boyhood I suffered from the lack of two things,—sleep, and Birds custard, which I thought was tastier than nectar. I suppose I never asked mother to make gallons of it, or she would have done so —but it was something for which I then had a craving. Now I can afford unlimited custard, I don't eat it at all. Other foods which I considered delicacies were Palethorpe's sausages, which like every other sausage, has never regained its pristine perfection ; Hume's tinned salmon—and Skipper's Norwegian brisling in oil or tomato. Incidentally, there was current in those days a belief that the tomato was a cause of cancer. It was not shared by our family, for in the summer we had dozens of tomato plants with heavy crops of fruit on them, of which we ate heartily.

A task I liked was to cut the young gorse shoots for our cob Prudence. When enough had been cut to make a bale—a cord was formed into a sling and the bale was slung on one's back. But if the shoots were small and tender they were gathered into a heap on a *llywanen,* which was a large sack opened out into a sheet. The four corners were tied diagonally and the whole carried on the shoulder by means of the whin-fork. It was then fed into a chaff-cutter, for which operation, two persons were needed, one to turn the wheel with its two sharp blades, and the other to feed the gorse with a wooden fork along a trough into this dangerous machine. The heavy pungent smell of the bruised gorse, combined with the warm smell of a horse was pleasant. I remember how we treated the gorse before we had a chaff-cutter. We used big mallets, the heads of which were 2 feet in length with a diameter of about 6 inches. Both heads had a cruciform cutter secured to it, and so we chopped the gorse into small pieces with these rather clumsy implements. All smells need not be perfumes of Arabia in order to be attractive ; the smell or stink of Camembert springs readily to the mind.

A very cold job in winter was that of cutting a block of hay, *gwanhaf,* from the rick or hay-cock. First the thatch was removed—then any mildewed hay, after which one set to work with a huge bladed, pointed knife thrusting it down its whole length of about 20 to 24 inches into the consolidated mass of hay. It was sharpened by stropping it with a rough sand-stone of the same material that grindstones were made. When the cutting was done, the hay, fragrant as cognac if the harvest had been favourable, was carried to the cowshed by means of a pitchfork stuck into it. One always tried to get enough cut, to last a week. Looking back one wonders why the hay was not made into a stack close to the cowshed, or in a shed adjoining. The explanation no doubt was that there were other projects with a better claim on the limited amount of money that was available.

The young married women of today have no conception of the tight budgets within which their grandmothers had to work. My mother had what she regarded as an infallible system. The oak dresser, we called it *seld,* had the usual set of blue willow-pattern dishes on the shelves, which were fitted with hooks on which hung all sorts of jugs. Certain jugs were selected for a high purpose—a big yellow one contained the contributions towards the Rent of some fields, a smaller green one was the receptacle for the Rates, a pot-bellied jug was used to hold odd coins till they could be exchanged for a note—a Clearing-house jug. There were jugs which held the money to pay for culm, flour, meal, and maize from the mill, a new heifer, new footwear and the odd garment. On this dresser, too, stood a clock which nobody but Mother understood. She would not allow it to be regulated, although it gained 20 minutes in a week. At the end of each week she stopped the clock and boldly turned the minute hand back 20 minutes. The time in midweek she ascertained by her own brand of mental arithmetical progression, or as we always suspected, by Guess and by God. Receipts were scrupulously retained, being stuck through by a long wire hook with a round block of wood to prevent the papers dropping off. Several of these were kept on nails underneath the stairs, to rest there undisturbed till the next batch were due for filing.

The job of driving porkers to market was always done while I was at the Grammar School, by mother and me. These porkers were piglets grown to 7 or 9 score pounds from one of our own litters, or those bought in the pig-market when they were about 6 or 8 weeks old. Mother was always buying these young pigs called in Welsh *perchyll.* It was the custom for the seller to deliver, so we would go to meet his cart at the top of the *cwm*, for he could never get his cart down—and we would put one or two of them in sacks and carry them home. I can feel now their pointed tootsies pushing into the small of my back, and the warmth of their bodies percolating through. As soon as they were all transported into a pigsty a great feast of warm milk, breadcrusts, vegetables and slops awaited them, after which they burrowed with happy grunts in the masses of clean straw which was their bedding. After all they were genuine V.I.P.'s. The porkers were driven to the town where mother's cousin kept an Inn at the back of which were scales to weigh live-stock. We would start off at five-thirty in the morning, but I had to be in school by nine, and mother went in front encouraging the pigs to follow by dropping the odd acorn, and calling ' bee-uckes bee-uckes ', which was the sound they associated with food. All would go well till we met a motor-car, when with one accord they would turn tail and leg it back towards home, and the peaceful life they had left behind. The critical situation was well understood by kindly folk who would rush out with a sheet of corrugated tin or something similar to form a barrage in the path of Garadene-minded swine, while we were puffing up from their rear fervently praying ' they shall not pass '. Once again all of us would head for the town, the approach to which was down a steep hill. If the pigs turned back they were by now tired, and there were plenty of eager helpers. After the weighing came the paying—and mother always gave me a few bob. That was how I got my first dictionary, a Collins pocket dictionary I think it was—which for years was one of my most treasured possessions. While I proceeded to school and lessons, mother would have tea and gossip (*clonc*) with her cousin. She would then buy the family some ' treats '. Of these, and rated very high were Palethorpe's sausages, which tasted much better than those home-made. Why is it that the red apple in your neighbour's orchard is sweeter than all those in your own orchard—and why is the grass greener in the eyes of a bullock as he gazes over the hedge—and why do we persistently believe there is a better place further on ? Perhaps humans as well as animals need this stimulant, which must be a form of escapism from boredom.

I was about sixteen when Father came home feeling very ill. He had been riding and training horses all day, and had been soaked to the skin. The doctor was called, and in a few days he diagnosed rheumatic fever. For a while my father was delirious, but this subsided with the crisis. One night I was sitting by his bed when he asked me to get out a Bank-book which was in the top left hand drawer of a chest. He asked me how much was in the deposit account, and I told him that at the last adding-up it was £105 with a few shillings and pence. He said that he was not sure of recovering from this illness, but if he did not, I was to use some of the money to go to the University. He took it for granted that mother would agree. This had the effect of making me feel that I was now the effective head of the family, and that it was time I became its bread-winner. As soon as the summer term was over I went as grocery assistant to one of the best shops in town. I had been helping there on Saturdays, and with the call-up of men over eighteen, they were glad to get, as I told mother, an intelligent lad like me. Mother was at first upset, and kept on asking whether it was what I wanted to do. I told her I was going to work very hard, have my own shop and become a millionaire ! We did work hard—from 8 a.m. till 9 or 10 at night. The chief provision hand, Mr. Jones, who was absolutely first-class at his job, was called up, and as he had taught me nearly everything I knew, I was soon worth more than the wages paid to me. I could bone hams or gammons—slice sides of bacon by hand, cut huge cheddar cheeses into manageable pieces, and guess the weight a customer asked for, without having to keep hacking off slivers to get it correct. We blended tea and Mr. Rees the ' boss ' would set us to work during the week on the chores for which we had no time on Saturday, which was the market day. These included cutting the red tea paper into the correct sizes for ¼, ½, ¾ and 1 lb. packages. The various blends of tea would be put into huge cannisters, and then weighed, packed and stacked ready for sale. Long bars of yellow soap, which came in one cwt. boxes from Bristol, would be cut into blocks ; currants, raisins, and sultanas were put through the cleaning machine ; sugar,—loaf, crystal, granulated, castor, pieces and demerara had to be weighed and stacked ; dog biscuits weighed into convenient packages ; tinned fruit and meat checked, and all ' blown ' ones discarded. Everything that would save time on Saturday was done beforehand. On Saturday the customers would be in the shop from eight onwards. The farmers would bring in eggs and butter, and had their value set against their grocery order. They left their baskets into which we packed the various goods they had ordered. A boy on a bicycle would take these laden baskets to the Inn of their choice, where the innkeeper and his wife would see that the farmer received them safe and sound. It was a mad rush all day till about nine in the evening. Then just before closing time the poverty-stricken women who lived in the slums came for their gubbins—for although a small town of only 3,000 inhabitants, it had two squalid streets where the birth rate was higher than anywhere else and poverty rife. When human beings become so poor that they have to forego even vital necessities, sex is still free, and so they add to their poverty by increasing their family at depressingly regular intervals. These people came with a few coppers, and we gave them off-cuts of American belly bacon, which was the cheapest, and broken biscuits which we could not sell to the ordinary customer. I saw to it, that by 10 o'clock when we shut the doors, a clean-sweep had been made of these unconsidered trifles.

Finally father was moved to Swansea hospital, where his sister Mary, who lived there, was able to visit him daily. I became the man about the house, the Boss, the Gaffer. By Good Friday I had set most of the garden, which was a big one, for father was a professional gardener. I had always helped in the garden, and knew what to do. The short manure was in the big midden heap by the cowshed three hundred yards directly above the garden up a very steep sloped terrace wood. Mother and I filled corn sacks with this manure, after which we tied them firmly and rolled them down the steep slope. They ended by a gap we had made in the garden hedge. This was a great labour saving device. The summer was dry, and the hay crop light. Again mother and I went into conference, and decided there was no point in waiting any longer for the rain, so we had the hay cut. The next day it rained, and continued for three weeks. We did all we could to save the crop by stooking it, but in the end all we had was a pretty mouldy cock of hay. Poor mother was worried lest father should blame her—but he did not. Altogether he was fifteen months ill, and he emerged from his ordeal a wreck of his former athletic self—with his heart badly affected. He could no longer deal with young spirited thoroughbred horses, so to play himself back to some sort of fitness he trapped rabbits for farmers with whom he shared the profit on a fifty-fifty basis. This paid reasonably well, and he put on some of the weight he had lost. He was then invited in the spring to become the head gardener at a neighbouring mansion, and this was his job for many years till he died at the age of 70. The cause of his death was a defective heart resulting from the rheumatic fever.

When the Michaelmas Term began in September, I was cleaning the windows of the grocer's shop when all my old pals passed by, exchanging some badinage and many congratulating me on release from bondage. In my heart I knew where I wanted to be, and when Christmas came I went to Dr. Rees and asked to be re-admitted. He agreed on condition I caught up with the Term's work I had missed. I gave in my notice, worked till the last Saturday of the vacation, and with a new cap on my head I returned to school. I was given a double quantity of Latin, Chemistry and Maths, but it had no ill effect ; on the contrary I came top of the form. Every Saturday I went back to the grocer's shop where from 8 a.m. to 10 p.m. I worked for the sum of six shillings and a quick snack. I was considered to be a trained hand by this time, and spent quite a time on the provision counter, boneing hams, lifting ribs and trimming big sides of smoked Wiltshire bacon. Then came the first slicing machine, a Berkel, or some such make—and bacon or ham could be sliced as thin or as thick as the customer required. I was very much *persona grata* at this shop for as long as I remained in the district.

Meanwhile the war was not going well for us, and in spite of my liking for the Navy, in which several of my cousins were serving, I was now mad keen on flying an aeroplane. I wrote to the R.A.F. Recruiting Officer who at once sent me a warrant to go for an interview to Haverfordwest, which I attended. They were apparently satisfied, and arranged for me to have a warrant to go to Cardiff for a Medical Board the day following my last examination paper for the London Matric. So to Cardiff to the Medical Centre in Newport Road, where for a whole day we proceeded from one test to another without a stitch of clothing on. One of the tests I still remember. Three medical officers stood side by side with their hands behind them. One of them suddenly hurled a missile attached to a long string. I did not know that the string was of a length calculated to stop the thing just short of the victim's face, so as it approached I fielded it, and with the same motion hurled it back at the thrower, who was too surprised to do anything about it. His two companions laughed heartily, and congratulated me on what they said were good reflexes and quick reactions. From Cardiff I went home, and waited for the travel warrant. I was now in His Majesty's Armed Forces. A farewell party was organised in the Chapel, and I was presented with a copy of the Bible in Welsh, and I think some pound notes. The atmosphere was emotional, reminiscent of an Irish wake, for the War was going so badly, with the casualty lists so long, that the dear old things could have been forgiven for feeling that here was another of their sons, who would not be alive long. One old lady was not at the meeting—but a day or two later when I was on my way to the station with a warrant in my pocket for London—she heard me clomp down the hill past her cottage and she came out to say goodbye, squeezing two half-crowns into my hand while shaking hands, and wishing me a safe return. This gesture moved me deeply, for Ann was not rich ; she was a widow with a crippled son, and in those days there was no pension to which she was entitled. She just worked here and there. The money she earned was most frugally laid out. As I trudged towards the station I thought of another poor widow who had contributed two mites of whom Jesus told his disciples that *pro rata* she had cast more into the treasury than any other person. So, followed by affection and love on all sides, I was on my way to my war, and unlike so many, I was looking forward to it. The fact that the days of the fighting man were as grass, was of no importance at all. Youth was wonderful, luminous, impervious, and the poet's warning that it did not endure could not penetrate to the quick. However ugly or filthy war was, it was still the supreme Adventure, and it was in this buoyant romantic mood that I went to have my first taste of it.

' O for yesterdays to come ' (Ed. Young, *Night Thoughts*)